# COPING WITH EXECUTIVE STRESS

# PRETEST

CW00358156

| | | | |
|---|---|---|---|
| **1** | Life has always been full of stress-producers—*stressors*—but stressors today differ from those of the past. | TRUE ☐<br>FALSE ☐ | Page 9 |
| **2** | In the work place change is the most ubiquitous stressor. | TRUE ☐<br>FALSE ☐ | Page 10 |
| **3** | How you cope with stress is less important than reducing the frequency and severity of stress episodes. | TRUE ☐<br>FALSE ☐ | Page 15 |
| **4** | There is no real difference between pressure and stress. | TRUE ☐<br>FALSE ☐ | Page 39 |
| **5** | Stress can be looked on as any disturbance which causes the body to make adjustments. | TRUE ☐<br>FALSE ☐ | Page 43 |
| **6** | Stressful work over a period of several weeks, or sometimes even just days, inevitably exhausts the body's capacity to cope. | TRUE ☐<br>FALSE ☐ | Page 48 |
| **7** | Trouble with one's boss can be more stressful than injury or illness. | TRUE ☐<br>FALSE ☐ | Page 53 |
| **8** | Stress may be associated with positive events such as promotion and personal achievement. | TRUE ☐<br>FALSE ☐ | Page 52 |
| **9** | A major characteristic of executives prone to heart attack (Type A) is that much of their stress is self-imposed. | TRUE ☐<br>FALSE ☐ | Page 64 |
| **10** | Type A executives have more than double the risk of heart disease as less-driven executives (Type B). | TRUE ☐<br>FALSE ☐ | Page 67 |
| **11** | Stress has almost no effect on blood pressure. | TRUE ☐<br>FALSE ☐ | Page 75 |
| **12** | The irritable bowel or irritable colon is the most common reason for abdominal discomfort and is chiefly due to stress. | TRUE ☐<br>FALSE ☐ | Page 89 |

**13** Peptic ulcer is often referred to as "the executive wound stripe." TRUE ☐ FALSE ☐ Page 92

**14** Stress is the major initiating factor in tension headaches but plays little or no role in migraine. TRUE ☐ FALSE ☐ Pages 103–104

**15** Most backaches involve muscle spasms rather than "slipped" discs, and stress can sometimes trigger these spasms. TRUE ☐ FALSE ☐ Page 111

**16** Neck pain commonly derives from muscle tension caused by stress. TRUE ☐ FALSE ☐ Page 115

**17** Relaxation exercises help little to relieve neck pain. TRUE ☐ FALSE ☐ Page 116

**18** There are two kinds of anxiety, one of which—trait anxiety—involves an individual's susceptibility to anxiety under stress. TRUE ☐ FALSE ☐ Page 123

**19** Tranquilizers should play a key role in the treatment of stress-induced anxiety. TRUE ☐ FALSE ☐ Page 125

**20** Mental depression, if brought on by stress, is immediately recognizable. TRUE ☐ FALSE ☐ Page 136

**21** Most depressions are brought on by stress events. TRUE ☐ FALSE ☐ Page 140

**22** It is possible for depression to produce many physical symptoms such as headache, dizziness, visual disturbances, heart palpitations, digestive difficulties, and reduction or loss of sexual drive. TRUE ☐ FALSE ☐ Pages 138–139

**23** Negative thought patterns, activated under stress, are involved in depressive states, and changing these patterns can be enough to overcome depression. TRUE ☐ FALSE ☐ Page 178

**24** Excessive caffeine intake can be solely responsible for anxiety or depression in some people. TRUE ☐ FALSE ☐ Page 144

**25** For many executives the "political" climate in their company is the most stressful job condition. TRUE ☐ FALSE ☐ Page 21

**26** A major cause of stress is worry and uncertainty over the company's or industry's future. TRUE ☐ FALSE ☐ Page 23

**27** For executives the most frequent stressors away from the job are financial worries, problems with children, and physical injury, illness, or discomfort. TRUE ☐ FALSE ☐ Page 25

| | | | |
|---|---|---|---|
| **28** | The most common complaint among executives' wives is, "My husband never talks." | **TRUE** ☐ **FALSE** ☐ | Page 37 |
| **29** | The personality traits of successful executives tend to hinder their recognition of when stress is getting out of hand. | **TRUE** ☐ **FALSE** ☐ | Page 37 |
| **30** | Onset of middle age, at about 40, can be a particularly stressful time for many executives. | **TRUE** ☐ **FALSE** ☐ | Page 35 |
| **31** | Resistance, from both men and women, to women in leadership roles is often a source of stress for the woman executive. | **TRUE** ☐ **FALSE** ☐ | Pages 153–154 |
| **32** | Most women executives do not consider their family responsibilities a source of stress. | **TRUE** ☐ **FALSE** ☐ | Pages 155–156 |
| **33** | While most working women would prefer part-time employment, that is not true for women executives. | **TRUE** ☐ **FALSE** ☐ | Page 160 |
| **34** | Working women have to expect a higher incidence of heart disease than housewives. | **TRUE** ☐ **FALSE** ☐ | Pages 162–163 |
| **35** | By tuning out their bodies and going on automatic pilot, executives can deal effectively with stress. | **TRUE** ☐ **FALSE** ☐ | Page 170 |
| **36** | A striking feature of executives who cope well with stress may be the ability to postpone thinking about problems until it is appropriate to deal with them. | **TRUE** ☐ **FALSE** ☐ | Page 173 |
| **37** | The bottom line of stress management is, "I upset myself." | **TRUE** ☐ **FALSE** ☐ | Page 178 |
| **38** | Stress immediately follows not a situation but rather what one tells oneself about that situation. | **TRUE** ☐ **FALSE** ☐ | Page 179 |
| **39** | Exercise should be avoided as an antidote for stress-induced problems. | **TRUE** ☐ **FALSE** ☐ | Page 183 |
| **40** | If one exercises to reduce stress, it is necessary that the exercise be vigorous activity. | **TRUE** ☐ **FALSE** ☐ | Page 188 |
| **41** | Taking quick, deep breaths in times of stress can be valuable for producing relaxation. | **TRUE** ☐ **FALSE** ☐ | Page 188 |
| **42** | Relaxation breathing may head off an oncoming tension headache or an attack of lower back pain. | **TRUE** ☐ **FALSE** ☐ | Page 189 |

**43** To relax muscles—a valuable stress-combating maneuver—you have to tense them first.

TRUE ☐
FALSE ☐
Page 191

**44** TM—transcendental meditation—is easy to learn.

TRUE ☐
FALSE ☐
Page 194

**45** The Relaxation Response can be as effective in combating stress as TM.

TRUE ☐
FALSE ☐
Page 195

**46** Given the nature of relaxation techniques, there can be no harm in them, even if you overdo their use.

TRUE ☐
FALSE ☐
Page 198

**47** Biofeedback may be valuable not only for many headaches but also for anxiety.

TRUE ☐
FALSE ☐
Page 202

**48** The objective of modifying Type A behavior is to achieve, or come close to achieving, a Type B pattern.

TRUE ☐
FALSE ☐
Page 203

**49** A vital need, if Type A behavior is to be modified successfully, is determination to make major changes quickly and dramatically.

TRUE ☐
FALSE ☐
Page 205

**50** Combating stress successfully depends on some kind of formal psychotherapy.

TRUE ☐
FALSE ☐
Page 208

**Answers:** 1. true  2. true  3. false  4. false  5. true
6. false  7. false  8. true  9. true  10. true  11. false
12. true  13. true  14. false  15. true  16. true
17. false  18. true  19. false  20. false  21. true
22. true  23. true  24. true  25. true  26. true
27. true  28. true  29. true  30. true  31. true
32. false  33. true  34. false  35. false  36. true
37. true  38. true  39. false  40. false  41. false
42. true  43. true  44. true  45. true  46. false
47. true  48. false  49. false  50. false

# COPING WITH EXECUTIVE STRESS

Other books available in this series

- EXECUTIVE  FITNESS
- EXECUTIVE  NUTRITION  AND  DIET

# COPING WITH EXECUTIVE STRESS

## Executive
## Health
## Examiners

## Richard E. Winter, M.D.
### Series Editor

**McGraw-Hill Book Company**

New York   St. Louis   San Francisco   Auckland   Bogotá   Guatemala   Hamburg
Johannesburg   Lisbon   London   Madrid   Mexico   Montreal   New Delhi   Panama
Paris   San Juan   São Paulo   Singapore   Sydney   Tokyo   Toronto

## The Author

Lawrence Galton is one of the most prolific medical/scientific writers in America today. As a medical columnist for FAMILY CIRCLE MAGAZINE and a contributing medical editor to PARADE MAGAZINE, Mr. Galton has contributed articles to over 50 national publications including READER'S DIGEST and THE NEW YORK TIMES. He has written or contributed to 19 books on health. He has received awards for his work from several associations, including the American Heart Association.

1 2 3 4 5 6 7 8 9 0   DODO   8 9 8 7 6 5 4 3 2

ISBN 0-07-019862-4

This book was set in Zapf Book Light by Progressive Typographers; the editors were Robert P. McGraw and Maggie Schwarz; the production supervisor was Jeanne Skahan; the designer was Murray Fleminger. R. R. Donnelley & Sons Company was printer and binder.

See Acknowledgments on page 210.
Copyrights included on this page by reference.

Library of Congress Cataloging in Publication Data
Main entry under title:

Coping with executive stress.
   (Executive health series)
   Includes index.
   1. Job stress.   2. Stress (Psychology)
3. Executives—Psychology.   I. Executive Health
Examiners.   II. Series.
HF5548.85.C66        613'.088658        82-15209
ISBN 0-07-019862-4                    AACR2

# Executive Health Examiners

| | |
|---|---|
| Richard E. Winter, M.D. | *Chairman* |

| | |
|---|---|
| William S. Wanago, M.D. | *Senior Vice President of Medical Affairs* |
| John A. Rossa, M.D. | *Director, New York Executive Clinic* |
| Allyn Kidwell, M.D. | *Director, Morristown Executive Clinic* |
| John M. Hill, M.D. | *Director, Stamford Executive Clinic* |
| Gazanfer Alkaya, M.D. | *Director, New York Stock Exchange Clinic* |
| Charles Ulrich, M.D. | *Director, Ambulatory Health Service Clinic* |
| Neil Crane, M.D. | *Director, EHE Washington Bureau* |
| Julio Rivera, M.D. | *Director, Occupational Medical Service, NIH Clinic* |
| Barbara Wasserman, M.D. | *Director, Clinical Medicine, NIH Clinic* |
| John Foulke, M.D. | *Director, NASA Goddard Clinic* |
| Richard Ross, M.D. | *Director, Fairchild Republic Clinic* |
| Gitanjali Mukerjee, M.D. | *Director, Spofford Detention Center, Medical Service* |
| William McBride, M.D. | *Director, NASA Dryden Research Center, Medical Service* |
| Fred Block, M.D. | *Director, Chemical Bank Clinic* |
| Frank Marzullo, M.D. | *Director, Bank of New York Clinic* |
| Donna M. Hartl, M.D. | *Director, Johnson & Higgins Clinic* |
| Riska Platt, M.S., R.D. | *Director, Nutrition Programs* |
| Steven Tay, M.D. | *Associate Director, New York Executive Clinic* |
| Jack Goldman, M.D. | *Associate Director, New York Stock Exchange Clinic* |
| Socrates Fotiu, M.D. | *Associate Director, NASA Goddard Clinic* |
| Stanley Craig, M.D. | *Radiology* |
| Stanley Halprin, M.D. | *Cardiology* |
| Lawrence Koblenz, M.D. | *Gastroenterology* |
| Stephen Krasnica, M.D. | *Cardiology* |
| Mauro Mecca, M.D. | *Internal Medicine* |
| Bernard Nemoitin, M.D. | *Proctology* |
| Jasu Sanghvi, M.D. | *Gynecology* |
| Erasmo Sturla, M.D. | *Endocrinology* |
| Sidney Wanderman, M.D. | *Proctology* |
| Mel Weinstein, M.D. | *Internal Medicine* |
| Madeleine Steele | *Project Coordinator* |

# CONTENTS

# PREFACE

Twenty-five years ago, in one of our preeminent medical research centers, there resided a group of very special laboratory animals. Challenged constantly, forced to make decisions and to act under pressure, they were the "executive monkeys." In one famous experiment, two monkeys were placed side-by-side in chairs equipped to give electric shocks. One of the monkeys—and only one—could prevent the shocks to both itself and its partner by pressing a lever. Under the psychological stress of being responsible for pressing the lever, this executive monkey developed duodenal ulcers.

The close correlation of behavior patterns in animals and humans has been thoroughly documented by scientific research. It has been shown that information obtained from animal research can be successfully applied to human research and experience. The study of animal behavior, for example, can result in a better understanding of the behavior of the individuals who go out each day to lead our governments, industries, and unions.

Few of us have ever watched chimpanzees in their natural habitat, the jungles of Africa. If we could observe these animals, we would see that they wander around, nibbling a few nuts here, a few berries there, eating continuously in small amounts. What they do *not* do is neglect eating for long periods and then pour raw alcohol onto the tender mucosal linings of their stomachs. They do *not* smoke several cigarettes, and thereby increase the outpouring of hydrochloric acid. They do *not* then consume large quantities of food, try to exist on insufficient sleep, and undergo rapid changes in environment. If they did, they would very likely suffer the same fate as a number of American executives under observation at a major research center who, possessing one or more of these habits, died before the study could be completed.

Medical science has accumulated an enormous amount of significant data from studies on animals and humans. As always, though, the important task is putting that knowledge to use in practical ways that can most benefit humankind. EXECUTIVE HEALTH EXAMINERS was founded more than twenty years ago for the primary purpose of making medical knowledge available to a particular group—executives. Over the years our medical staff has examined executives from every kind of business and profession and at every level. From this vast experience it has become apparent to us that these executives—men and women alike—are often *simultaneously* exposed to all the life-threatening habits that chimpanzees naturally avoid. And it is this circumstance that, in our opinion, makes executives unique. Other groups are, of course, subjected to some of the same threats to their health, but, in our experience, only in the executive lifestyle do these threats converge at the same time.

The conviction that executives are unique, that their lifestyles are different and therefore their health needs special, led us to prepare a series of books specifically for executives. In these volumes we combine solid medical fact with our years of professional experience to provide practical, proven approaches to solving health problems. Each volume deals with an area of health where executives are especially vulnerable. COPING WITH EXECUTIVE STRESS provides the most current medical information on stress and its effect on both the mind and body to show executives how to recognize and cope with stress in executive life. EXECUTIVE NUTRITION AND DIET is a commonsense program for nutrition and diet that has been highly successful for thousands of executives. All the special problems of executive lifestyle are dealt with in this basic, balanced discussion of sound nutritional habits and healthy diet. EXECUTIVE FITNESS is a flexible, workable exercise program designed for busy executives. Within a basic format, it offers a wide variety of exercise options, all of which are certain to result in increased stamina and productivity.

There is no question that the demands of executive life make good health maintenance difficult. Having guided hundreds of thousands of executives to positive and lasting changes in their lifestyle, however, we know that the habits of eating properly, exercising regularly and coping with stress can be successfully acquired. The volumes in this series offer sound information gained from long and specific experience with executives. We view these books as a kind of survival kit for executives. It is our hope that they will enable every executive to enjoy a longer, healthier, more productive and satisfying life.

Richard E. Winter, M.D.
*Chairman*

# INTRODUCTION

**A**s an executive, you have to cope with stress; there is no escape. Stress is as much a part of the business world of today as the annual report. It's felt by the young man or woman driving upward, by the middle-aged executive whose career may have peaked, and by the person at the top with heavy responsibilities.

Of the thousands of businessmen and -women we see at Executive Health Examiners each year, as many as 20 to 25 percent show evidence of stress and stress effects. And the stress-related symptoms of at least 5 percent are serious enough to require professional help.

For the businessman or -woman, how can stress be anything but virtually unavoidable, considering the ever-mounting complexities, uncertainties, and pressures of business, often coupled with complex family, economic, and social factors?

When stress gets out of hand, it can create potentially serious damage. At the least, it may lead to irritability and a lowered threshold for anger or frustration. But sometimes it is incapacitating, provoking anxiety or depression. Physically, it can trigger or exacerbate a wide variety of disorders: hypertension, heart disease, ulcer, colitis, and more.

Stress, however inevitable, nevertheless is widely misunderstood. No concept dealing with human functioning and health has produced more confusion. According to conventional wisdom, stress is to be avoided if at all possible. But it cannot be. And even if it were, its avoidance would probably be calamitous to the individual and to society.

The need is not for stress evasion but for effective ways of coping with stress. We know that such methods are achievable, and we need to find out more about them.

From our work with men and women at Executive Health Examiners, we have become convinced of the need

1

for a concise book, free of jargon and addressed specifically to executives, about living with stress and coping with the kinds of stress faced by managers.

To that purpose, this volume is dedicated. May it help executives at all levels to handle stress successfully in their business and family lives.

**1**

IF A MAN NEGLECTS EDUCATION
HE WALKS LAME TO THE END OF HIS LIFE.
PLATO, CCCLXVII B.C.

LIBERTY WITHOUT LEARNING IS ALWAYS IN PERIL·
LEARNING WITHOUT LIBERTY IS ALWAYS IN VAIN·
JOHN F. KENNEDY, MCMLXIII A.D.

# WOULD YOU CALL THEM STRESS VICTIMS? ARE YOU ONE?

**A**lthough he does not look it or even know it, R.G. is a victim. At 41, a division manager in a packaged goods company, he appears calm, assured, on top of his job. Yet he has frequent attacks of neck pain. They come as often as weekly and last usually a day or sometimes two days. They can be relieved to some extent with analgesics, especially when the drugs are coupled with heat and massage. The pain, R.G. is certain, is simply the result of awkward sleeping positions he must be getting himself into.

N.D. is a victim, too. A 37-year-old executive in a financial firm, dynamic, ambitious, dedicated to her work, she appears to be happy in it. Her only concern: every once in a while she suffers from an eczematous rash. Starting with small patches on the backs of her thighs, it weeps, itches, and spreads. It responds to her self-treatment with salves and ointments, usually with the help of a weekend she devotes to complete relaxation. She is allergic to something, she thinks, but no allergist has been able to pin down the culprit.

5

At 46, L.B.R. has just become vice president in a large corporation. Married for 14 years, he has three children, the oldest just reaching adolescence. His new job requires considerable traveling and he has increased his time at work. His having less time to spend with his family has led to tensions at home.

As alienation develops, he experiences some concern over his diminishing libido. L.B.R. has an extramarital affair but it arouses feelings of guilt. More and more, his job performance suffers. A major new special project, to which he has contributed significantly in the planning stage and to which he has expected to be assigned, is given to someone else.

He suffers from insomnia. He takes sleeping pills at night, "uppers" and megavitamins in the morning. But he becomes more and more moody, irritable, depressed. Less than a year after his promotion, he experiences chest pains for the first time. By the end of the year, he is drinking excessively and his marriage is on the edge of divorce. His 13-year-old daughter is arrested for the possession of marijuana.

Fourteen months after his promotion, he has a heart attack, which he survives.

Are these three persons stress victims? Very much so. And they are only three among millions of such victims.

If stress is not the *most* significant, common, and far-reaching influence on health and well-being in the United States, it ranks high.

## "A Bewildering Array"

The United States Clearing House for Mental Health Information recently reported that the nation's industry has had a $17 billion annual decrease in its productive capacity over the last few years because of stress-induced mental dysfunction. Other studies estimate even greater losses (upward of $60 billion) arising from stress-induced physical diseases.

In 1977, a study done by the National Science Foundation concluded:

Stress is a major problem in the contemporary United States. It negatively affects the daily lives of scores of millions of

# If stress is not the *most* significant, common, and far-reaching influence on health and well-being in the United States, it ranks high.

Americans. It causes a bewildering array of physiological, psychological and social malfunctions. On an economic level, the effects of stress probably cost the nation over $100 billion annually. Moreover, available evidence suggests that stress-related maladies are on the rise.

In the scientific literature of just the last 5 years, the number of study reports on stress has almost doubled, now totaling more than 200,000 entries.

Stress can affect people at all levels. For executives alone, one estimate has it, American industry is losing as much as $20 billion annually in lost workdays, hospitalization, and early deaths caused by stress reactions.

## Today's Problems "Squeeze and Clutch"

We have seen a drastic change in the nature of sickness in recent decades.

Throughout the eighteenth and much of the nineteenth centuries, much of illness was ascribed, even though somewhat vaguely, to the mind—largely to despair and melancholy. Then Pasteur and Koch showed that germs cause disease. One after another, they and their colleagues and successors identified and began to conquer infectious organisms. Out of these advances grew scientific medicine. It was mainly concerned, at first, with all the bacteria, viruses, fungi, and other organisms capable of producing disease. And, indeed, the once-terrible infectious scourges—diphtheria, typhus, smallpox, and the like—have largely vanished. They are no longer to be found in any modern list of leading causes of serious illness and death.

Yet doctors are busier—and hospitals are fuller—than ever.

Consequently, in recent years medicine has had to take another hard look at disease causes. This look has led to a growing recognition of the role of stress.

* *It is late at night. You're walking home through city streets. You become aware that you're being followed. You walk faster but the footfalls behind you tell you that you are not gaining ground. Except for your followers, the streets are deserted. You don't know who is following you. You are afraid to turn around.*

    *Stress!*

* *It's a beautiful morning. You arrive at work, park your car in the space reserved for you, walk to your office, full of cheer. You belong here. In a dozen years, you have moved up the corporate ladder. You have a beautiful home, kids in private schools, and bright (you think) prospects ahead.*

    *But now on your desk you find a note from the executive vice president. "For possible economies," it says, "we're considering the consolidation of several divisions. Please make a study of any advantages there might be in merging your division with X processing."*

    *You feel your face flush, your pulse pound. You experience indignation, even rage, a vast upsurge of need to be physically violent against an enemy—change. But, in view of what you see as a potentially major threat to your career, to your getting where you want to go and where you thought you were going, you have to maintain calm.*

    *Stress!*

There are many stressors—both initial causes and contributing influences—that lead to stress. Life is full of them.

"Almost everyone we know is tense and uptight at different times because of one damned thing or another. Life crowds in on us, its problems squeeze and clutch, and we all try somehow to cope," observes Dr. Leonard Cammer, a distinguished psychiatrist.

> For executives alone, one estimate has it, American industry is losing as much as $20 billion annually in lost workdays, hospitalization, and early deaths caused by stress reaction.

## Not New, Yet Very New

Stress itself is certainly nothing new. Primitive people had their stressors—mortal combat with foes, problems of getting enough to eat, among others.

Our pressures today generally differ from those of our ancestors.

We may not face the threat of jousting with fierce animals, but we know the threat of criminal attack on the streets. In the United States, 1.3 million cases of violent crime were reported in 1980. There were 101 major crimes per 1000 persons recorded in New York City, property crimes as well as violent offenses, and this figure is exceeded by rates of 114 per 1000 in Phoenix, 129 in Newark, 143 in St. Louis, and 157 in Miami.

Even if we do not confront them in person and on the scene, we are, with our virtually instantaneous communications, almost constantly aware of threats and actualities of wars and other catastrophes wherever they occur. They do not leave us free of anxiety or disturbing dreams.

Has the machine age been kind to us? Has the automobile, for example, given us many advantages? Is it a source of joy—or stress—when you find yourself trapped in traffic on the Long Island Expressway or any of its many equivalents?

Industrialism has brought us change—and change can be stressful.

Yesterday's world was relatively stable. To be sure, change took place. There is always some change. But in yesterday's world, new things came along at a slower pace.

There was opportunity to assess them and their impact. We could become accustomed to them before another change had to be faced. In recent years, changes have been coming so fast that we may have lost much of our ability, individually, to adapt.

The communications overload to which we are exposed provides so much information and so many sources of information that, as often as not, the result is confusion and, with it, sometimes also a sense of insecurity.

Today's world is one of social upheaval. Once, many social institutions, marriage among them, gave form and structure and provided some stability to our lives. Today, they may no longer do so because of changing norms and patterns.

Conflict develops between parents and children. To some extent, it always has done so. But now, teenagers, backed by peer pressure and even prodded by it, reject parental values outright. Is there an "empty nest" syndrome, which affects some families when children, having grown up, move out? At the same time, are not other families experiencing a "crowded nest period," when children are grown but not yet out of the home?

Value systems are changing. Hoodlums are on the streets in vast numbers. Vandalism is commonplace. Immorality appears to be all too usual among public officials. The quality of goods and services seems to—and often, in fact, does —deteriorate. Discourtesy appears to be almost the norm.

## "The Most Ubiquitous Stressor"

Change has been called the *most ubiquitous stressor* in the work setting.

It's easier, obviously, to adjust to what we consider beneficial than to what seems threatening. But, in fact, an expectation of change, whether good or bad, can be stressful, perhaps even more so than the actual change itself.

Many executives face not only the drastic change involved in loss of a job, but also the change, perhaps somewhat less drastic, of relocation—or of merger, takeover, or divestiture. Let a new executive assume command at the top

# THE STRESS OF CHANGE

To say we live in a world of change is to say the obvious. We take for granted the enormous changes happening around us and within us all the time: changes in technology as computers do more and more work that was formerly done by people; changes in values as the traditional conceptions of family and religion are challenged; changes in economic conditions with inflation and recession; changes in the environment, with pollution becoming an ever-growing problem; changes in families as children grow up and leave home; changes in individuals as they age.

We seem to encounter something of a paradox in talking about this process of change. On the one hand, we say that without change, there is stagnation and death; on the other hand, with change can come instability and chaos. We say that with change comes progress, yet with change also come anxiety and stress.

Our society is quick to recognize the positive effects of change but slow to acknowledge and deal with the stresses and instability that invariably accompany it. There is no doubt in my mind that a significant part of the vague uneasiness and apprehension that so pervade our society is the result of all the changes taking place around us that we cannot control.

It's easy to become overwhelmed so that we either throw up our hands and feel there is *nothing* that we can control, or we rigidly hang on to what we have, fearing that even that will be lost. It's no wonder that people tend to resist change, and the more unstable a person's life, the more desperately he clings to what he has even if what he has isn't very good.

John C. Connelly, M.D.,
The Menninger Foundation

Change has been called *the most ubiquitous stressor* in the work setting.

# Any expectation of change, whether good or bad, can perhaps be even more stressful than the change itself.

and, almost inevitably, changes occur down the line, sometimes markedly altering management style. And other kinds of changes in the workplace—new equipment, new materials, new products, new job classifications—may be disconcertingly stressful.

Dr. Elliot Jacques, head of the Brunel University School of Social Institutions and a social-analytic consultant to industry, has observed that

No matter what the economic or social system, wherever technology requires a common work task, wherever more than a few people must work together toward a common goal, we have to have a bureaucratic hierarchy.

But most management structures are mismanaged, says Jacques, and "don't utilize the individual's total creative energies; as a result they cause unnecessary stress and tension." Jacques goes on:

> In the United States, more than 75 percent of the working population is packed into bureaucratic hierarchies. On balance, these hierarchies—as managed or mismanaged at the present time—*do* change negatively. It's an understatement to say that uncertainty about a job, having your future career assessed by someone else, being dependent upon the work of others in order to discharge your own responsibilities, finding the nature of your employment organization changing without having a say, and not having any way of being sure of equitable and fair reward are each a source of anxiety. In combination, they are sources of chronic tension.

## Stress Effects

Stress, a normal part of life, is not all bad. It may account for a lot that gets accomplished in the world.

It's another matter, however, when stress becomes too great or continues at a high level too long—and when the individual cannot cope with it effectively. It is then that stress becomes disturbing.

It can have many effects. It can trigger a physiological arousal mechanism—a series of nervous, glandular, and other reactions that involve many body systems and that may become manifest as symptoms. They may mimic symptoms of a variety of diseases, such as chest pains, palpitations, hot and cold spells, chills, shaking, insomnia, headache, musculoskeletal pains, diarrhea, choking sensations, and others.

Stress can produce an organic or a physical reaction—exacerbating an already present disease or setting the stage for a new one. It may lower natural resistance and thus allow infection or another pathological disturbance to develop.

Nor are these effects all that may occur.

Dr. Jeremiah A. Barondess, president of the American College of Physicians, has noted that

> Stress today is not only the most common factor in the symptomatic ills that bring people to their physicians; it is also a

# THE HUMAN COST OF STRESS

The human cost of stress has been acknowledged . . . at least since the 1930s and 1940s, when American industry was hit by an epidemic of executives dying of heart disease. Since then, stress has been linked to hypertension, coronary disease, migraine and tension headaches, peptic ulcers, renal disease and asthma. Doctors believe unrelieved stress can lead to depression and general anxiety, to alcoholism and drug addiction, and to a breakdown in normal relations with friends, family and colleagues.

Kathy Slobogin
*New York Times Magazine,*
November 20, 1977.

major factor in predisposing, initiating, and sustaining organic disease. It may bring on emotional changes that may become so severe that they keep a person from functioning efficiently and from carrying out the responsibilities of his or her particular role in life.

Dr. Barondess added this significant note:

Unfortunately, in our society "physical illness" is more respectable than "mental illness"; symptoms believed to be physical in origin are more acceptable to most people than symptoms thought to be of emotional origin. Patients therefore tend to endure the consequences of stress while they're mainly emotional or psychological—and usually they don't see the doctor until they think they're sick in the more conventional sense—that is, physically. At that point, the patient's welfare depends very heavily on the physician's understanding of stress and its consequences, of how these consequences manifest themselves, and of how to differentiate the patient's symptoms from those of true organic disease.

## The Curious Phenomenon

Stress makes some people tick; it sickens others. K.W. is a woman who, in her mid-thirties, has come up the organizational ladder fast—*very* fast. Recently placed in charge of rescuing a losing operation that was seemingly headed nowhere but down, she has huge responsibility. She dotes on the pressures. She is at work by 7 A.M., rarely leaves until far into the evening, and usually works Saturday. Her phone almost never stops ringing.

"My day," she says, "is very long and pressure is very much a part of my job. The pressure of responsibility, to make the operation profitable, the pressure of being a symbol of what women can do. But I need pressure to function

## Stress makes some people tick; it sickens others.

—the more the better. It's what I run on. It motivates me."

L.M. has a different problem. He was moving up well in the company, handling one assignment after another effectively, taking the usual pressures and some unusual ones as well. Then he landed in a position under a boss who disturbs him intensely. "He makes petty demands, changes his mind constantly, and makes his job far bigger than what it really is. He makes me smaller than what I am. He wants to make me over—in his own image."

L.M. comes home at night exhausted, frazzled. He can offer his wife and kids only irritability. He feels his guts constantly tied in knots. He gets headaches—agonizing ones. He controls his feelings on the job, but it takes tremendous effort. He sticks, sickening with the stress.

It's a curious phenomenon, stress. Serious enough for anyone, very serious for some people. It's curious, too, in what it really is (there are many misunderstandings about it), the mechanisms involved in it, the marked differences in the ways in which it can affect different people.

There is growing conviction among many investigators that how people cope with stress is far more important than the frequency and severity of stress episodes. Some people cope remarkably well—almost as if by instinct. But there are other factors involved in effective coping, and they can be understood and put to use by others. They will be our concern in this book.

## THE EXECUTIVE MONKEY EXPERIMENT

The experiment with the executive monkeys is a classic one. It involved strapping pairs of monkeys to chairs and administering electric shocks to them at intervals. One of the monkeys in each pair—the "executive"—was given charge of a device that could turn off the current to avoid shocks for himself and his partner. Both monkeys of the pair got exactly the same shocks. They were discomfited to the same degree. But it was the "executive" monkeys in the experiment who developed ulcers—and died of the ulcers. Their partners stayed ulcer-free and alive.

The one difference between the monkeys in each pair was that the executives were under the stress of continual vigilance and decision making while the partner was not.

Stress can lead to depression and general anxiety, to alcoholism and drug addiction, and to a breakdown in normal relations with friends, family, and colleagues.

## THE PRICE OF DENYING STRESS

If you hold your breath beyond your capacity while swimming underwater, you begin to panic. Your anxiety is triggered because the brain gets a warning of serious threat to the body from the respiratory system. Immediately, the brain issues orders for escape.

But the brain can trick itself, and such self-deception can underlie many stress-related disorders, including ulcers, asthma, heart disease, and high blood pressure, according to Dr. Gary E. Schwartz of Yale University.

In *Psychology Today*, Schwartz reports on an experiment he and his colleagues carried out with a group of forty men whose self-perceptions represented three types of anxiety. Fifteen claimed that they were seldom anxious and were nondefensive about their feelings; they were labeled "true low anxious." Fourteen others said they were not anxious but did acknowledge being defensive; they were labeled "repressers." The other eleven men were very anxious and willing to admit it; they were labeled "true high anxious."

All forty were put through a moderately stressful free-association test requiring them to complete a series of partial sentences, some aggressive in tone, some sexual, some neutral. At the same time, their heart rates, sweat gland activities, and forehead muscle tension—all indicators of anxiety—were recorded.

Just as they had claimed, the fifteen "true low anxious" men showed only moderate stress. The fourteen "repressers," however, had extreme body responses indicating high anxiety; some of their reactions were even more extreme than those of the eleven men who had reported feeling high anxiety. Such self-deception, Schwartz believes, may interfere with the normal biofeedback which enables the brain to regulate body functions.

Normally, for example, the brain gets messages about blood pressure from nerves sensitive to pressure changes. If the messages indicate high pressure, the brain tells the heart to slow its beat and calls on blood vessels to dilate. Both responses will help to lower pressure. Interference with this process is what Schwartz calls *disregulation*. "But why," he asks, "should the brain act in this seemingly self-destructive way? One possibility is that high blood pressure offers people a short-term advantage in stressful situations."

When, for example, Rockefeller University experimenters injected rats with a drug to elevate blood pressure, they found that the animals gradually became less sensitive to electric shock and less motivated to escape it. Humans, the experimenters speculated, may develop hypertension in a similar way, in response to persistent stress. By always denying feelings of anxiety, frustration, or anger under stress, people may gradually condition themselves to raise their blood pressure.

"Messages from the arteries calling for lowered pressure," observes Schwartz, "would then be short-circuited in the cortex and ignored, until high blood pressure becomes habitual."

Schwartz's final conclusion: While the usual approach is to use drugs to treat high blood pressure—and there is a place for such intervention—the medicines often treat effect rather than cause. More promising may be measures to make people more sensitive to their bodies and capable of controlling pressure consciously, and other measures to help them handle a threatening environment in ways that make it less stressful. "In the long run," he says, "we may be better off trying to modify the causes of stress than tuning out the body's danger signals."

# THE STRESS IN EXECUTIVE LIFE

It's hardly a matter of time alone—although the hours add up. As a group, according to U.S. Department of Commerce figures, executives average $47\frac{1}{2}$ hours of work a week, not including time spent in local or long-distance travel and in business-related entertainment. Of the executive group, 38 percent work 49 hours or more, and 22 percent of women and 42 percent of men executives exceed 49 hours.

There may be better definitions of executive work, but one describes it quite concisely as "the specialized work of maintaining an organization and operation . . . a system of cooperative effort."

In such "effort," there is plenty of opportunity for stress.

The work may be intense and demanding: keeping an organization functioning as smoothly as possible; dealing with many events, changes, and details; delegating work; getting others to perform effectively.

In a perceptive book, *The Executive Parent*, S. P. Hersh, M.D., former assistant director of the National Institute of Mental Health, remarks:

> An executive's world is best described as one of input overload. Facilitator, overseer, synthesizer, and sometimes builder and creator of new activities, the executive is committed to work of the most intense, preoccupying kind. Executive work can devour energy and time in gargantuan amounts. . . . Without empathy, without pity, and without ultimate grati-

tude (despite salaries and special awards), the system voraciously demands more and more.

Hersh outlines what he calls the "normal challenges" that can be expected to occur in the course of each executive's work life. They include suddenly assigned added tasks; demands for greater output and/or higher quality of performance; new jobs or assignments; moves within the organization or moves at company request to other communities; "as well as various kinds of negative actions that a corporate system or other system may impose on an individual (demotions or withholding of advancement)."

Obviously, such challenges can become crises. As Hersh notes, their significance as tests of talents and tensile strength depends on many factors, such as the state of the individual's physical and emotional health and the kind and status of family and other support systems.

Moreover, functioning on the job can be affected by challenges in personal life: marital problems, children's behavioral problems, family health problems, drug problems, alcohol abuse, serious accidents.


## What Is Stressful?

### *Executive Perceptions*

Several recent studies have focused in illuminating detail on executive stress.

One, made for the American Management Association by Ari Kiev, M.D., professor of psychiatry at Cornell University Medical College, and researcher Vera Kohn, covered 2659 executives in top and middle management. Asked to choose among a substantial variety of possible sources of stress, both top and middle managers agreed on four leading causes:*

*Ari Kiev, M.D. and Vera Kohn, *Executive Stress: An AMA Survey Report*, New York: AMACOM, a division of American Management Association, 1979.

* *Excessive workload and unrealistic deadlines*

* *Disparity between what the executive accomplishes and what he or she would like to achieve*

* *The company's general "political" climate*

* *Lack of feedback on job performance*

According to almost three of every four of the executives at both top and middle levels, the most stressful situation was the one that occurred most frequently: work demands and time pressures.

Typically, executives reported having "a number of projects due for completion in a very short time," and with pressures from above and from clients, yet with shortage of support staff, executives need to devote long hours to the assignments, with little or no chance to delegate. They reported understaffed departments "for level of proposed business we handle" and "justification of additional people impossible without first landing the work to support them." They also reported frustration at getting assignments and deadlines which prevented them from producing an end-product of the quality required.

Fully 60 percent of the executives at both top and middle levels considered highly stressful the disparity between company expectations and their own individual goals. If

In a report, "Coping with Mental 'Wear and Tear,'" published in *Occupational Health and Safety* (October 1980), Dr. Steven H. Appelbaum, professor of management at Concordia University, tells of conducting several stress workshops with 350 health care administrators and 160 middle-management executives of a multinational chemical corporation.

Fifty-five stress factors were identified by the 500-plus individuals involved in the workshop sessions. Both groups agreed during separate sessions that there were 30 factors causing stress which were job-related and 25 others to be found "within the individual."

# STRESS FACTORS: JOB-RELATED —OR WITHIN THE INDIVIDUAL

## Job-Related Factors

1. Need to work fast
2. Work overload
3. Ambiguous roles
4. Inadequate information
5. Vague objectives
6. Role conflict
7. Job dissatisfaction
8. Responsibility for people
9. Lack of job security
10. Obsolescence
11. Early retirement
12. Too little responsibility
13. Being redundant
14. Relationship with boss
15. Relationship with colleagues
16. New supervisor or subordinates
17. Status incongruency
18. Under- or overpromotion
19. At career capacity
20. No input into decision
21. Performance evaluations
22. Time constraints
23. Competition, not cooperation
24. Closed organization climate
25. Quality of work life
26. Major changes in policies
27. Management by crisis
28. Sociopolitical constraints
29. Inability to delegate
30. Leadership style incongruencies

they found some security in being with an organization, it apparently could be offset significantly by frustrations over unmet needs and lack of self-fulfillment.

As for "political" climate, one of every two executives taking part in the study made a point of noting that any company where the prevailing atmosphere creates the impression that "it's not what you do but whom you know" is a stressful place to work.

"I am very confident in my own ability yet fear the politics," one executive remarked. Another, confessing anxiety

## Factors within the Individual

1. Low self-esteem
2. Workaholic
3. Financial problems
4. Compromised values
5. Family demands
6. Marriage
7. Relocation and mobility
8. Hidden agenda
9. Emotional health
10. Conformity, submissiveness
11. Rigid personality
12. Competitiveness
13. Overaggressiveness
14. Impatient, pressured
15. Frustration
16. Ambiguity
17. Feeling threatened
18. Lack of control
19. Low self-actualization
20. Death of family member
21. Serious illness
22. Low social support
23. Fear of success or failure
24. Inability to ventilate
25. Inability to let go

after being told by his management that he needed more development before he could take on a job he wanted and felt he could handle immediately, said: "The real anxiety lies in my feeling that something political is really the reason."

Quite understandably, lack of feedback on job performance ranks high as a stressor. With no clear idea of whether there is any approval of the way a job is being done, it's difficult to feel confident and at ease. Surprisingly, the study found that "the percent of organizations in which there is inadequate communication between superior and subordinate is quite high."

## *Other Stress Factors*

As you might expect in addition to the top four causes of stress, many others were described by executives participating in the Kiev-Kohn study.

Particularly among middle management, lack of authority to make decisions that matched responsibilities was a common sore spot. Of the 1237 middle-management executives in the study, 39 percent found this stressful. But so did 30 percent of top management.

A relatively common worry among top management (for 36 percent) was uncertainty about the company's or industry's future. That possible anxiety bothered only 20.8 percent of middle management. Nor was this worry solely a matter of a company's financial position. As one executive put it: "A proposed change involving the promotion of a person in whom I have little confidence as a manager has me concerned about my job satisfaction and the future of the company."

Almost 30 percent of both top and middle management found an unsatisfactory working relationship with a superior to be a source of stress.

As you might foresee, subordinates can be sources of stress. But so can colleagues. Surprisingly, the executives found their colleagues even a bit more stressful than their subordinates.

Subordinates become stressors, for example, when they fail to perform well after being promoted by the executives

concerned, when they leave in the midst of a major project, when they do such poor work that it becomes necessary to fire them. Colleagues become stressors when their failure to meet their own responsibilities creates problems elsewhere as well.

Still other stress factors were reported in the study. Uncertainty about what actually was expected on the job was of concern to slightly more than 24 percent of top management and almost 28 percent of middle management.

Company reorganizations or changes in structure bothered about one of every four executives in both top and middle management. And lack of advancement opportunities, or limited ones, meant stress for about one of every six executives in top management and almost one of every three in middle management.

## Private Stress

Executives, of course, face stress in their private as well as their professional lives.

What are the most frequent stressors away from the job? According to the Kiev-Kohn study, the three most common types are also the three most stress-provoking. They are: financial worries (not surprising, suggest the researchers, considering inflation leading to a concern "not so much for job security as for asset security"); problems with children; and physical injury, illness, or discomfort.

# More Stress Perceptions

### 300 Executives in 12 Companies

At an international symposium on the management of stress held in Monte Carlo, Dr. John H. Howard of the University of Western Ontario reported on a recently completed study in which 300 managers from 12 major companies were asked what they found to be the principal sources of stress on the job. Analyzing their responses, Dr. Howard found four general characteristics of executive jobs that seem most stress-producing:*

*A Feeling of Helplessness* Executives often see problems, understand them, find reasonable solutions for them —yet find themselves unable to act because of organization constraints. As Howard notes, feeling unable to influence a situation can be extremely stressful; power—the ability to act—is a great antidote for stress.

*Overwork* The sheer quantity of work is a common problem. Executive jobs often are characterized by "much work at an unrelenting pace."

*Urgency* Actually, Howard looked into this characteristic in a separate study and found that, "on average, managers do something different every 7 minutes. Their jobs are characterized by brevity and fragmentation and stress."

*Ambiguity and Uncertainty* Often, problems are not clearly defined; company policies are also ambiguous. When

---

* John H. Howard, Second International Symposium on the Management of Stress, Monte Carlo, November 18−22, 1979.

# The three most common types of stresses are: financial worries, problems with children, and physical injury, illness, or discomfort.

there is considerable uncertainty, decision-making is difficult.

These characteristics—"the major underlying dimensions of stress in a manager's job," Howard calls them—originate in a number of different situations, according to the study.

## The Situations

Howard categorizes the troublesome situations thus:

**Poor Management or Boss** This tops the list of stress sources, in the view of the 300 executives in the study. They pointed to lack of planning and direction along with chronic indecisiveness as causing the most tension. They also noted poor communications, often caused by a failure by top management to communicate total plans.

**Lack of Authority or Blurred Organizational Structure** It is most frustrating to be given an assignment and the responsibility for implementing it—and then to have no authority to properly carry out the job. This ranked as the number two stressor. Blurred organizational structure was defined in terms of unclear job descriptions and too many bosses.

**Promotion and Recognition** Uncertainty about future promotion and frustration for lack of praise and recognition from top management were considered to be significant stressors by many executives. Many complained they had no idea of the criteria by which they were currently being judged or what were supposed to be the prerequisites for the next position up the line. As some put it, they often don't know which "hoops to jump through."

***Basic Work Problems*** These problems, common in virtually all businesses, include constant telephone interruptions, meetings that take up too much valuable time, and the inability to find time to concentrate on a single problem long enough to solve it.

***Company Politics*** Always a source of stress, office politics most often plays a role in promotions, transfers, division of authority, and allocation of supplies and equipment. Among the comments was this one: "There is a type of 'buddy' system among top management as they are very protective of each other. This results in the wrong people in key jobs and the right people in a position of no authority."

***Personnel Problems*** These problems center not only on employees unsuited to their work but also on the difficulty of handling personal problems of employees.

***Volume of Work*** The need for heavy volume, combined with insufficient time and inadequate staff, can be stressful, and in more ways than one. "Most managers," notes Dr. Howard, "initially blame themselves for this lack of time. They often see their inability to adequately delegate work as the culprit. However, after considerable soul searching, managers come to realize that it is frequently an impossibility to complete all the work. It is only with this realization that the situation can be solved or coping strategies devised."

***Change*** Some executives consider any change to be stressful. Others point in particular to unfamiliar work, jobs, people, and moves.

# Executive Stress:
# A Psychologist's View

Dr. Herbert Krauss, consulting psychologist for Executive Health Examiners, was asked for his observations on stress in executive life, and based on his experience with executives he sees in consultation, he replied:

"One of the difficulties I have found, particularly with middle-level executives is that frequently they are pushing paper across the desk. And they wake up one morning and figure out that they are pushing paper and that their worth is judged by the amount of paper they push.

"And they are worried about that. Worried because they are successful, they have perks, their kids are in the right schools. But by some definitions they are nonfunctional. They are not producing a concrete product. They are producing an idea. The idea can change. Somebody else can come in on top of them, with a somewhat different idea of the way the business is going to go. Are they still going to be able to push the paper?

"The middle-level executive often has the problem that he is implementing somebody else's ideas and those ideas can change drastically, quickly. He has a lot at stake in the game and he is somewhat cut off from the decision-making process and he doesn't know sometimes what tomorrow will bring.

"The middle-level executive can have another problem. And that is, where is he going? Is he moving up? Or is he moving laterally? And if he is moving laterally, how is he going to deal with that as he sees people go up over him? He sees people buying and selling around him, himself getting older, and he is bought and sold, and there is, he may think, nothing left.

"Lower-level executives, on the whole, are running. At the middle level, you can run. But my experience has been that at the lower level there is an enormous amount of running . . . getting things done . . . being active . . . looking and feeling effective.

"Often, the need to look and feel effective is in areas or fields in which you don't have the responsibility to allow you to be effective. So there may be continual strain between what you know you must accomplish to get even to the middle level and your ability to do so by yourself. And the politics may be enormously difficult. You may find, in some companies, that you are in an extraordinarily competitive environment with no friends, working very very hard, with your family life deteriorating, and with the feeling that the only way to move on is to be narrower and stronger and more ruthless.

"Family life may deteriorate because of the changes in

temperament that may occur. I mean, it is very hard to be a shark in one place and not to be a shark in another place—at least it is for most people.

"It is very hard to get used to telling others, all day, what to do and then, in the evening, walk into a place in which you have to relate warmly. It can be extraordinarily hard to have to be organized all day and then walk into a house which, if children are involved, may be defined by chaos.

"And so the guy wears himself out by day; he comes home; he wants some support; he wants to be patted on the back for doing a good job. The wife, too, wants support; the kids go a bit wild. And the way people often tend to cope with this kind of situation is the way they cope in business: trying to exert control, trying to preserve order. But really what is needed are modulation and problem solving."

## At the Top

"What of stress at the top-most levels?" we asked.

Dr. Krauss replied, "It can be there, and it can be some-thing quite different." He continued:

"Here are people who may have given up a great deal to get where they are, or are going, or have been. They have played a game very well that generally is not played well—a game of power. Not all people by any means can play that game very well for a long period of time without wearing down or without suffering from it.

"For perspective, take a step back with me for a moment. A French sociologist, Emile Durkheim, at the turn of the century talked about modern industrial society as being anomic

It is very hard to be a shark in one place and not to be a shark in another place.

> **It is very hard to get used to telling others, all day, what to do and then, in the evening, . . . walk into a house which, if children are involved, may be defined as chaos.**

and egoistic. Durkheim suggested that modern industrial society becomes increasingly anomic and egoistic.

"Anomie, of course, means a state of society in which normative standards of conduct and belief have weakened or disappeared. In primitive societies and farm societies, there is close regulation of individuals. They have a place, a role, and that role is integrated throughout the society. You know who you are. There is a great deal of regularity. There are limits to ambition. There are also limits to freedom.

"Now we move into industrial society. There are no limits to anybody's behavior. Durkheim talked about 'sickness of infinity,' which is produced by this anomic, competitive, egoistic trend. In such a society, there are enormous rates of suicide, murder, and loser-ism. They are almost built into the system.

"How do you cope with stress in a no-longer status-fixed, competitive, anomic society? Whom do you turn to as a friend? Where is your center of value—in a society where you can be bought and sold like a commodity, where you can be waved away—goodbye—after perhaps 20 years of effort?

"The products of this kind of society tend to be less material. I mean, most of the products have relatively little to do with really eating a meal or taking care of one's self. Most of our products have to do with ideas: the 'ideal' meal, the 'fashionable' meal. And what that does is build in an enormous range of change.

"And so you have a sociologist like David Reisman talking about 'other-directed' people. You see them in New York: today, they all look this way; tomorrow, another way.

"Executives have the same experience. Tomorrow, it will

be this way; next day, we'll have zero budgeting; the day after, something else. And where is the center of the individual!

"And societal institutions weaken. Durkheim made a large analysis of divorce and suicide rates, for example. And what he found is still true: societies in which divorce is easier have higher suicide rates. Not necessarily because marriage is pleasurable but because marriage *regulates;* it sets people through their motions; it doesn't open them up wide to the chaos of unreality. And that is what we all face in this society. There is almost nothing in New York, for example, that is impossible. One has to be on guard at all times. What streets you take, how you look at other people, how you hold yourself—we are almost always available for something random to happen.

"Well, Durkheim and almost everybody after him suggested that one of the things that characterize relatively stress-free living is regularity. Without regularity, most people are lost. Because much of what we think about ourselves comes to us from others. And if there are no stable "others" in our lives, or if the information they are continually giving us is different, it is almost impossible to have a sense of stability.

"So Durkheim talked about the destabilization of modern society which can produce enormous stress—all kinds of stress-related disorders in one group of people, psychosis in a second group, suicide in still another group.

"The other issue Durkheim identified is egoism—everybody doing their own thing. And to whom do you turn for aid, for companionship, for stable love if everybody is doing their own thing!

"When it is every person against every other person, anything can happen to produce instability. The individual is left isolated and to his own devices. And most isolated individuals don't have much chance. Oh, maybe 5 out of 1000 can live by themselves. But most can't. And even those five need some kind of minimal contact.

"When you are hurt, just to be able to talk to somebody, to think it through in the process of talking, even just to get it off your chest, means something. So now we have a 'shrink' industry—because with what friend can you talk!

"If you are free, then almost anything is possible for you

—and if anything is possible, then it is very difficult to find a sense of value.

"So some top-level people, the people who are free, who have clawed their way up (even those who are competent, depending on the point of view), who have come to realize that they are operating in a world of artificial meaning, look about and they can have everything they want, and nothing seems to matter. Some pretend things do matter—power matters, being king of the cesspool matters, ordering people around matters.

"But nobody in human history has considered such matters to be higher motivations, or complete motivations.

"People come to me all the time in my clinical practice and say 'I am tired of living.' And I ask the successful ones, Why? Often they say, 'Well, there is nothing for me to do.' I say, 'But look at the streets; there are poor people dying on the streets of New York City. You could spend a lifetime being involved in meaningful work for other people. And often their response is: 'That wouldn't do anything for me.'

"You'll recall that the distinguished psychiatrist Alfred Adler argued that most neuroses, most characterological disorders, of a mild or moderate degree, can be attributable to lack of societal interest.

"To the extent we become isolated and singular and 'rational' to the exclusion of everything else, to the extent we become just power- and object-oriented, we cut our own throats. It happens all through society.

"Is achieving those goals which executives typically may achieve at the top seen as a sign of success? Do they 'have it made'? The evidence is coming in that while they may have made it socioeconomically, still, when it comes to living a better life, a fuller life, and to having some sense of meaning, many have much the same problems, in different forms, that the rest of us have. And sometimes, like the rest of us, when they win, they lose.

---

# Societies in which divorce is easier have higher suicide rates.

---

"Some know they lose and seek help. Some don't know and they may drink, or play around, or give other people a hard time, and become caricatures of living human beings. And then they produce the 'walking wounded.'

"So lots of times in clinical practice, the people we end up seeing are the people who are lost but don't know what they have lost, or how."

D.S., a 50-year-old vice president of personnel for a large corporation where he had been working for 20 years, is a good example of someone who "found" himself again. He earned a generous income and had a substantial benefit package and a happy home life. He was outwardly quite secure. He had been receiving annual health exams at Executive Health Examiners (EHE) for a number of years, and had generally been considered healthy. Although his health status was unremarkable, this year he raised a number of questions with his EHE physician, a doctor who had seen him for a number of years. D.S. was concerned that life had become too routine, too predictable. His relationship with his wife was stable and friendly, but without excitement. He saw no further opportunities in his current job situation, and was unchallenged by his responsibilities. In addition, he was physically inept, and complained of impotence. Thorough examination revealed no underlying medical cause, thus pointing toward a psychological origin. Also noted was an increase in alcohol consumption from his usual one to two drinks a day to four or five each day.

The doctor felt that D.S. was suffering a characteristic example of midlife crisis. The doctor, convinced that D.S. needed a "new outlook on life," discussed his potential for personal growth and enhanced self-image without discarding the personal security and stability that he had established by years of hard work. Communication with his wife had declined because their mutual interest for so many years had centered on the children, who now were grown and no longer in the home. Therefore, an effort was made to find a solution that would bring D.S. closer to his spouse as well as to his work.

D.S. and his wife remembered that when they were first married, they were both animal lovers and had toyed with the idea of breeding show dogs. However, between jobs and family responsibilities, this idea was forgotten. Soon, they

> To the extent we become isolated and singular and rational to the exclusion of everything else, to the extent we become just power- and object-oriented, we cut our own throats.

were excitedly working together to rekindle this mutual interest; within a year, they were breeding show dogs and entering competitions with some luck. Within 2 years, they were heavily involved as officers in the local kennel club. Now their life has taken on new meaning along with new friends. Alcohol is no longer an incipient threat to D.S., and he and his wife are quite compatible in every way. Fortunately, they were able successfully to work through his "midlife crisis."

## Midlife Transition

But you do not have to be over 50 to experience a midlife crisis. For many, it comes earlier.

As young executives move along in their early thirties, they often experience some reorientation in attitudes. Some begin to question their value and to wonder whether their drive to get ahead is really worth the effort. Many grapple with the idea of a possible change of career. And, commonly, there is increasing concern with "making it," a more intense recognition that how far they can advance in their thirties may have very much to do with their ultimate success.

As they get beyond 35, many of the ambitious become impatient at not moving ahead fast enough. They may intensify their efforts to get promoted. And some become increasingly resentful, and even depressed, because they are seemingly not appreciated.

The onset of middle age, usually put at about 40, often is a stressful time.

For many, as psychiatrist Theodore Lidz, M.D., has put it, the start of middle age "is ushered in by several difficult years that have been termed the midlife crisis or midlife transition.

> The crisis is not set off by any significant event but, rather, by the realization that more time stretches behind than stretches before one. The balance of life is upset by awareness of the limits of life's span, and there is apt to be a recrudescence of existential anxiety concerning the insignificance of the individual life in an infinity of time and space.
>
> Two of the world's literary masterpieces start on this note. The Divine Comedy opens with the lines, "Midway in the journey through life, I found myself lost in a dark wood, having strayed from the true path." Goethe's Faust finds that although he has studied philosophy, medicine, and law thoroughly, he is fundamentally no wiser than the poorest fool, and he makes a pact with Mephistopheles in an attempt to salvage something in life.

At the start of middle age, Dr. Lidz notes, there is still time to make changes, perhaps even to start afresh, or at least to make the best of the years remaining. But there can be no further delay.

So, commonly, middle age is a time of stocktaking, of assessing how life is going to turn out. "Will dreams be fulfilled? Must one come to terms with getting by?" Dr. Lidz

# The onset of middle age, usually at about 40, often is a stressful time.

asks. "Or must one accept disillusionment and failure?" Then he observes:

> However, the stocktaking concerns more than external success. It has to do with inner satisfaction and the hope of achieving a sense of completion and fulfillment. Are achievements compatible with one's ego ideal derived from early expectations? How great are the disparities between one's way of life and what provides a sense of self-esteem? For some, middle age brings angry bewilderment because neglect of meaningful relationships in the striving for success makes life seem empty.

## The Three Questions Faced at Midlife

Stanley H. Cath, M.D., professor of psychiatry, has, as a primary clinical interest, emotional disorders in middle and later years of life. In his view,

> It is paradoxical that at the midpoint of life when one is confronted by a very personal meaning of aging through the aging and death of one's parents, one's own decline is counterpointed by the emergence, if not exploding into life, of sexuality and creativity in one's offspring. Most families experience these developments as a critical challenge of transition, albeit in slow motion. As a common heritage, the decades after age 35 contain at least three questions.

* *With whom do I live, age, and relate in this way?*

* *How much longer do I have to live at my best, or to correct my ways?*

* *How will I age, with what human supports, and how will I die —with integrity or despair?*

Every reflective human being goes through a series of self-monitoring inventories and self-assessments, a life review, a reassessment of goals. . . . The task of confronting the self is enormous.

## *Loneliness and the Image*

The question in the Kiev-Kohn study was: Who is the person with whom you can talk about your personal internal problems and concerns?

Typically, 60 percent of the executive husbands answered thus: "I don't want to burden my wife. She does not understand my business problems and she wants to talk about the world when I come home. In fact, there is nobody I could really trust."

One executive even added solemnly, "And when I want to talk to my dog, he runs away!"

Yet the most common complaint of the executives' wives, that is, of 45 percent of the women questioned, proved to be: "My husband never talks. I hear about the things which happened from others weeks later at social meetings."

It's a fact that many executives, as they advance up the ladder and take on more responsibilities, become more isolated and independent at a time when they most need emotional support. Many balk at sharing their worries at home for fear of appearing weak or inadequate. The very personality traits that help to make for the successful executive—drive, combativeness, emphasis on individual strength and ability—can also make it hard to recognize when stress is getting out of hand. And they can make it still harder to seek help.

In many cases, there are symptoms that signal distress, including extreme irritability, sleeping difficulties, waning appetite for food or sex or both, frequent headaches, and periods of deep "blues." They may be so frightening that the executive feels they must be kept submerged.

And, too often, submerged they remain despite their effects on performance and productivity; sometime later, they become somatized into physical disturbances and can be treated as a "real illness."

# STRESS: WHAT IS IT?

**P**ick up almost any newspaper, magazine, or medical journal today and you are likely to read something about stress.

What, precisely, is this phenomenon which, we are often told, "has surpassed the common cold as the most prevalent health problem in America"?

In a way, we all know what it is, and yet we do not. The word *stress*, very often loosely used, seems to mean different things to different people. Many use it to connote both an external condition, loss of job, for example, and the body's internal reaction to that condition.

Among medical scientists, however, stress has to do with the bodily response. And any external conditions which arouse the response are considered to be *stressors* or stressful life events.

## IT STARTS WITH PRESSURE

Stress begins with pressure.

When we speak of ordinary pressures, we mean the daily routines, responsibilities, and chores that keep us going, usually in some kind of work schedule or what might be called a "social harness." They are stable expectations guiding or harnessing both work and recreation. These activities are the normal pressures of life—far too loosely called the "normal" stresses of life.

However, there is a fundamental difference between pressure and stress. *Pressure* is a stimulus, external or internal, to which we respond. *Stress* results from our perception of a need and our gearing up for the response. It is a coupled response.

Thus, one's need to rouse from sleep (perhaps this is the end of a "need" for sleep) is the pressure. The stress, if present (we awake late and must rush), derives from the way we perceive and respond to the pressure of wakefulness. A more functional term for this kind of pressure is *stressor*. Stress, if it occurs, appears in response to the stressor.

Engineers speak much more clearly about this. For them, stress is a structural response to a stressor, and strain is a kind of measure of the "tax" on the structure.

Daniel X. Freedman, M.D.
Editor of the *Archives of Psychiatry*.

## The Flow of "Juice"

Prehistoric people, we now know, survived because of the stress mechanism. That same mechanism works for us in primal fashion as it did for them.

Consider this situation:

You are relaxing after dinner, reading. Everything is quiet until, suddenly from another room, you hear a noise. Someone is moving about, and no one should be there.

You look up from your book. Without question, something strange is going on. You are about to get up when the door to the other room is flung open. Out rushes someone you have never seen before.

Instantly, striking physical changes are set in motion in your body. You were relaxed before, even somewhat drowsy after your dinner as more blood went to your gut to aid digestion and less went to your brain. You breathed slowly and evenly, your heart beat was slow and regular, your skin was dry and warm.

But now, digestion stops. Blood is shunted away from the gut to your brain, which is now highly aroused, and to your muscles, which are tensed for action. Your heart pounds, your blood pressure shoots up, and your skin (as the blood moves away from it, too, to feed brain and muscles) becomes cool and somewhat clammy.

A lot more is going on within you. Blood sugar (glucose) is released from storage in the liver into your blood: this is an extra supply that can be burned fast for energy. White blood cells flow into the blood from the spleen; they too are an extra supply ready to fight off infection. Your supply of blood platelets—tiny ovoid bodies in the blood—increases, ready to produce clotting in case of injury.

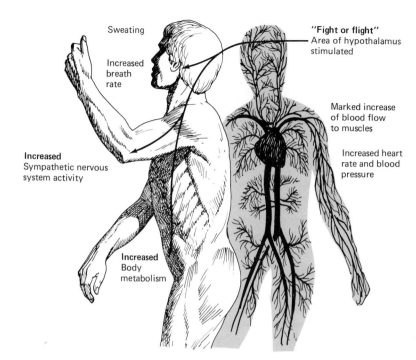

Sweating

Increased
breath
rate

"Fight or flight"
Area of hypothalamus
stimulated

Marked increase
of blood flow
to muscles

Increased heart
rate and blood
pressure

**Increased**
Sympathetic nervous
system activity

**Increased**
Body
metabolism

*Physiologic changes associated
with fight-or-flight response*

You have experienced an alarm reaction, a quick readying for flight or fight.

From your nervous system, a message has gone to the adrenal glands atop the kidneys to secrete a hormone, adrenalin, the "juice" that increases heart action and relaxes and enlarges the airways so more air can reach the lungs more quickly. In addition, adrenalin reaches the pituitary gland at the base of the brain, which responds to it by secreting hormones to cause the thyroid, parathyroids, and other glands to pour out their hormones, all to complete the almost instantaneous mustering of your body and mind forces to deal with the stress situation. These responses account for some of the seemingly superhuman feats of action that are often exhibited under stress.

It was Dr. Walter B. Cannon, a famed Harvard physician-researcher who, almost 70 years ago, established the facts of what goes on when stress occurs. Ever curious, Cannon had among his diverse interests a desire to know something about stomach movements. So he fed a cat a meal containing barium salts, which allowed the animal's stomach to be seen more clearly on x-ray film.

Studying films taken at various times, Cannon found that when the cat was undisturbed, the stomach showed wave-like digestive motions. But when the cat was frightened or angered, the motions stopped and did not resume for an hour or more after the cat no longer was aroused.

Cannon's work went further. With a cat strapped into a holder and frightened by a barking dog, Cannon looked for adrenalin in the cat's blood and found it. He also detected increased amounts of glucose in the blood. And the extra glucose spilled over into the urine and could be found there.

Did this finding apply to humans? Taking urine samples of Harvard students in the midst of tough exams, and also collecting urine samples from football players during an exciting game, Cannon found high levels of glucose, the result of adrenalin released in the heat of emotional strain and excitement. Even players on the bench showed similarly high levels.

## Homeostasis, a Nice Balance

Any organism, including the human body, tries to maintain internal balance.

For example, we need a certain amount of sugar (glucose) circulating in the blood to nourish tissues bathed by the blood. But not very much glucose—about one-sixtieth of an ounce for each pint of blood—is needed at any one time.

If, for any reason, an excess of glucose is present, fluid is drawn from tissues in the body's effort to dilute blood to overcome the excess glucose level. That will mean increased thirst to replace tissue levels of fluid. It will also mean frequent urination so that the kidneys can dispose of some of the excess fluid intake and the excess glucose spilling over into the urine. These, in fact, are early symptoms of diabetes, a state of hyperglycemia or high blood sugar.

On the other hand, if there is prolonged glucose inadequacy, we have hypoglycemia. This insufficiency can cause inadequate nourishment of tissues and, because the nervous system often is affected first, may lead to mental confusion.

Normally, the body makes sure that blood sugar concentration stays relatively stable no matter how much or how little sugar you may eat in a given day or how much energy you burn up. Let blood sugar fall below its proper level and the pancreas puts out a hormone, glucagon, which tells the liver to release some of its stored sugar. Other hormones as well get into the act to reestablish proper blood sugar levels.

Conversely, if blood sugar rises above normal levels, glucagon and other hormones are turned off and the liver, rather than release stored sugar, pulls more in for storage. And the pancreas secretes more insulin, which helps push glucose from the blood into muscles and fat cells. The body thus makes constant adjustments to achieve a normal balance, that is, a stable state known as homeostasis.

Stress can be looked upon as any disturbance which causes the body to make adjustments. It is certainly not all bad. The body is organized to make reasonable adjustments in response to stimuli or stressors. And, in fact, it can suffer for lack of such input.

We respond to normal sights, sounds, and other sensory perceptions. Take them away, and there is trouble. Volunteers have been placed in unlighted, soundproof cells. Almost always, the sensory deprivation produces distortions and even hallucinations. Memory is disturbed. So, too, is manual dexterity.

On the other hand, unusual stress can be injurious in diverse ways. Swedish investigators some years ago subjected a group of thirty-one soldiers, average age 29, to the stress of 3 days at the shooting range without being allowed to sleep, smoke, or take walks. Adrenalin secretion shot up. About 25 percent of the subjects showed abnormal electrocardiograms. One man experienced temporary panic, headache, blurring of vision, palpitations, and a pulse rate of more than 100 beats a minute.

## The Noxious Stimuli

It was Dr. Walter Cannon who introduced the term *homeostasis* to indicate the maintenance of internal balance. A monumental figure credited with doing much of the groundwork which helped to stimulate intensive research on stress, Cannon published his landmark book *Bodily Changes in Pain, Hunger, Fear and Rage* in 1929.

Cannon investigated how such emotions as fear and anger contribute to animal survival. He studied the stressful effects of pain and hunger. He demonstrated how the pouring of adrenalin into the bloodstream from the adrenal glands in an "alarm" reaction readied an animal for flight or fight. And he made the observation, too, that psychological stress could produce bodily changes that in time could lead to disease.

In 1953, Dr. Harold G. Wolff, another major contributor to the growing concept of stress, wrote his important book *Stress and Disease.* He investigated how people respond to stressful stimuli and defined such stimuli as being any influences that produce responses from such tissues as muscles, nerves, or glands or that increase any body function or process.

He considered that certain stimuli are "noxious." They can have damaging effects on individual body cells or tissues or on the health of the entire person. A noxious stimulus, he observed, can be not only a physical problem, such as a broken bone, but even a change in a human relationship which may have threatening connotations.

Wolff also noted that what may be a noxious stimulus for one person does not necessarily have to be noxious for another. Is one person demoralized, for example, by a serious illness which might, on another, stimulate positive, creative action? Such an illness, in the case of Charles Darwin, led

A noxious stimulus can be not only a physical problem, such as a broken bone, but even a change in a human relationship which may have threatening connotations.

him to the idea of evolution. Severe illness, too, stimulated Florence Nightingale to push for nursing reform.

## Hans Selye and Biological Stress

Unquestionably, Hans Selye, M.D., is a preeminent figure in modern stress research. He is currently president of the International Institute of Stress.

Selye is the scientist who has helped to give stress some of its modern meaning as what he calls a *nonspecific* response of the body to any demand upon it. He also established another basic concept—that of the general adaptation syndrome (GAS).

As Selye has pointed out, any demand made upon the body obviously is specific. If you are exposed to cold, you shiver to produce more heat. If you become hot, you sweat and the evaporation of the perspiration has a cooling effect. If you run up half a dozen flights of stairs, your muscles need more energy, so your heart beats more rapidly and strongly and your blood pressure rises to speed delivery of nourishing blood to the muscles.

Drugs and hormones also have their specific actions. A diuretic drug, a so-called water-pill, increases urine production; adrenalin augments pulse rate and blood pressure and at the same time increases blood sugar. On the other hand, insulin decreases blood sugar.

> Yet [says Selye], no matter what kind of derangement is produced, all these agents have one thing in common: they also make an increased demand on the body to readjust itself. The demand is *nonspecific*, it requires *adaptation* to a problem regardless of what the problem may be. That is to say, in addition to their specific actions, all agents to which we are exposed produce nonspecific increase in the need to perform certain adaptive functions and then to reestablish normalcy, which is independent of the specific activity that caused the rise in requirements. *This specific demand for activity as such is the essence of stress.*

It doesn't matter whether the agent or situation is pleasant or unpleasant. What counts is the intensity of the demand for readjustment or adaptation. In Selye's words:

The mother who is suddenly told that her only son died in battle suffers a terrible mental shock; if years later it turns out that the news was false, and the son unexpectedly walks into her room alive and well, she experiences extreme joy. The specific results of the two events, sorrow and joy, are completely different, in fact, opposite to each other; yet their stressor effect—the nonspecific demand to readjust to an entirely new situation—may be the same.

Is it difficult to see how such essentially different things as sorrow and joy, heat and cold, drugs and hormones can produce the very same biochemical reaction?

But there are everyday analogies, Selye points out. One example is the home in which heaters, refrigerators, bells, and light bulbs produce heat, cold, sound, and light quite specifically, yet depend for their functioning on one common, nonspecific factor: electricity.

Stress, Selye emphasizes, is not the result of damage. "Normal activities—a game of tennis or even a passionate kiss—can produce considerable stress without causing conspicuous damage."

## "The Syndrome of Just Being Sick"

Selye got a hint of what he was later to call stress when, in 1925, he was studying medicine at the University of Prague. In one of the lectures, students were shown several patients in early stages of various infectious diseases. The professor pointed out all the specific signs and symptoms characteristic of each disease. But what struck Selye was that each patient felt and looked ill, had a coated tongue, complained of diffuse joint aches and intestinal disturbances. The patients had a common syndrome, but the professor attached little significance to the signs common to all the diseases, since they were nonspecific and of "no use" to a physician in diagnosis.

"I saw," Selye recalls, "what appeared to be a 'general syndrome of sickness' superimposed on all individual disease, and I could not understand why my professor did not pay serious attention to it."

More than half a dozen years later, Selye had occasion to

think about that syndrome again. It was 1936 and he was working in the Biochemistry Department of McGill University in Montreal, trying to isolate a new hormone in extracts of cow ovaries. He injected the extracts into rats to see whether their organs would show changes that could not be attributed to any known hormone.

The extracts changed the rats in three ways: their adrenal glands enlarged; their thymus, spleen, and lymph nodes shrank; and deep, bleeding ulcers appeared in their stomachs and upper guts. The changes varied from slight to pronounced, depending upon the amount of extract injected.

At first, Selye thought that the changes proved that there was a new hormone in the extract. But he soon found that he could produce the same three changes by injecting extracts of kidney or spleen or toxic drugs.

Gradually, he began to realize that the reaction he was producing with his impure extracts and toxic drugs was an experimental replica of that "syndrome of just being sick" he had noted years before.

The three changes (later to become the basis for development of the stress concept) were described in a paper in *Nature* in 1936 as "A Syndrome Produced by Diverse Nocuous Agents." Subsequently, the reaction became known as the biological stress syndrome or general adaptation syndrome.

In that same *Nature* report, Selye suggested the name "alarm reaction" for the initial response, arguing that it probably represents the physical or somatic expression of a generalized call to arms of the body's defensive forces.

### The Three Stages

The alarm reaction, Selye determined, is certainly not the entire response. Rather, it is the initial response and can be followed by two other response stages, those of resistance and exhaustion.

In the first reaction of alarm, the brain recognizes the attack of the stressor, which may be anything from the approach of a lion to the appearance of a threatening memorandum in the office. It signals the pituitary gland to produce a hormone, ACTH, which, moving into the blood

> The brain recognizes the attack of the stressor, which may be anything from the approach of a lion to the appearance of a threatening office memorandum.

and reaching the adrenal glands, causes the latter to discharge adrenalin and other hormones. As a result, the three changes take place, and there are also effects on heart rate, blood pressure, sugar level in the blood, and other conditions.

If the stressor is extremely drastic, death may occur within the hours or days of the alarm reaction.

If the initial stage is survived, the second stage, resistance, follows. Now the fight is on—even when the body is, in effect, acting against the mind because the stressor is a psychological one. The body combats the stressor or hastens to avoid it and begins to repair the damage. The body has adapted.

But if the same threat or stressor continues for a prolonged period, the third state, exhaustion, develops. The capacity for adaptation is exhausted.

Our supply of adaptation energy, Selye believes, is finite. Once we use it up, we face senility and finally death.

We can, of course, endure stressful work for days, even weeks, and find resistance and adaptability restored after a rest. But chronic stress, year after year, eventually can use up all our reserves.

### Diseases of Adaptation

Since Selye first introduced the biological stress concept, there has been considerable progress in analyzing how hormones participate in stress reactions. Moreover, he now has concluded that various derangements in the secretions of these hormones can lead to *diseases of adaptation*—so called, he explains, because they are not directly due to any particular stressor but, rather, to a faulty adaptive response to the pressures induced by some stressor. Selye observes:

> In this sense, many ailments, such as various emotional disturbances, mildly annoying headaches, insomnia, upset stomachs, sinus attacks, crippling high blood pressure, gastric and duodenal ulcers, certain types of rheumatic or allergic afflictions, as well as cardiovascular and kidney disease, appear essentially to be initiated or encouraged by the body itself because of its faulty adaptive reactions to potentially injurious agents.

One question which undoubtedly occurs to you is this: Why should the same stressor—for example, a reprimand from a superior or a financial worry—cause such different lesions as ulcer in one individual, migraine in another, a heart attack in still another?

This, notes Selye, has been traced to conditioning. The conditioning can be internal, as by genetic predisposition, age, or sex, for example. It can be external, too; treatment with certain drugs or dietary factors are examples. "Under the influence of such conditioning factors," Selye writes, "a normally well-tolerated degree of stress can become pathogenic and cause diseases of adaptation which affect predisposed areas of the body selectively."

## Personality and Proneness to Stress

Not long ago, Navy medical investigators studied thirty-two pairs of identical male twins 42 to 67 years of age. One member of each pair had heart disease and the other did not, or one had severe and the other mild heart disease. Inheritance, obviously, could not be a factor; it was the same for both members of a pair.

The study looked hard, in particular, at four possible stress factors: devotion to work, lack of leisure, home problems, life dissatisfactions. It demonstrated that men who had experienced heart attacks were much more involved with their work than the other men were. It showed, too, that those with little or no heart disease were best able to relax away from work; those with more severe disease had more home problems, often centering on financial arguments; and the more severe the disease, the more the men were dissatisfied with their lives.

But another significant finding also turned up: even more important than work, leisure, and home-life patterns was how the individual subject viewed these and other areas of his life.

It appears from the study that someone who works long hours, takes relatively little leisure time, has domestic problems, and all the while enjoys life may not be so vulnerable to heart disease as someone with similar life patterns who is dissatisfied.

This finding accords with what Stewart G. Wolf, M.D., observed years ago about the coronary-prone individual: this person is like the mythologic Sisyphus who passed the time in Hell pushing a large rock up a steep hill and never quite getting to the top. The candidate for coronary disease, Wolf remarked, is a person who not only meets a challenge by exerting extra effort but also takes little satisfaction from accomplishment.

And Wolf's observation accords with the later delineation of the now well-known stressful Type A behavior, about which more later.

## A Scale of Stress Factors In Our Lives

Early in this century, Adolph Meyer, M.D., Johns Hopkins University, kept "life charts" on his patients. From these, he repeatedly found that his patients tended to get sick when clusters of major changes occurred in their lives.

Thomas H. Holmes, M.D, professor of psychiatry at the University of Washington School of Medicine, has built on Meyer's work. He drew up a list of events that seemed to play a role in triggering various illnesses: the common cold, skin outbreaks, colon diseases, tuberculosis. Some were negative events, such as being fired from a job or serving a jail term. But many were ordinary events, like a move to a new home, a new job, a promotion, a visit from an in-law.

# The candidate for coronary disease is a person who not only meets a challenge by exerting extra effort, but also takes little satisfaction from accomplishment.

Diverse as they were, they did have one thing in common: a change in life pattern. Holmes concluded that a person can get sick when something happens that calls for adaptive behavior or social readjustment, when coping requires effort that may weaken resistance to disease.

Holmes and a colleague, Richard H. Rahe, M.D., then gave 394 people a list of 43 life events ranging from a change in sleeping habits or trouble with the boss to marital separation or death of a spouse. The two physicians asked their subjects to rate the events as to the relative degree of adjustment called for by each.

The highest-ranking event, the one believed to provoke the most stress, proved to be the death of a spouse with a score of 100, as compared with marriage, which carried a score of 50. Others in the top ten were divorce, marital separation, a jail term, death in the family, personal injury or illness, marriage, discharge from a job, marital reconciliation, and retirement.

In further studies, individuals were asked to list by year for a number of years any major life events they had experienced. These lists then were compared with the individuals' medical histories. In case after case, the year in which several major life events occurred was followed by a year in which serious illness developed.

The greater the life change and burden of stress, the lower the body's resistance to disease and the more serious the illness that develops.

The death of a spouse is especially likely to bring on illness. Holmes and Rahe found that death is 10 times more frequent among widows and widowers in the year following the spouse's death than it is among all others in their age group. Also, a study in Sydney, Australia, showed that in the year following bereavement, 32 percent of a sampling of widows experienced a marked deterioration in health. Their illness rate was 16 times greater than that of married women of similar age and background.

Holmes and Rahe found, too, that divorced people, in the year following the divorce, have an illness rate 12 times higher than that of married people.

They also determined that the individual who accumulates a score of 300 stress points within one year has a 90 percent chance of becoming seriously ill or of having a major accident. If fewer points are experienced within one year, the odds of a major health change may be 50/50.

What is your score?

As you see, and as Dr. Holmes emphasizes, stress is not limited to negative change but may also be associated with positive events such as marriage, promotion, and personal achievement.

Even such positive events carry strain with them, however. Marriage is regarded as a happy event, yet bride and groom are under stress. Often, prior to marriage, people may have some doubts about their future spouse, themselves, and even the whole idea of marriage.

The man or woman who has worked at a job for a number of years will experience considerable anxiety and stress when suddenly promoted to a new position, even though the new role has been eagerly sought. Both the new vice president and the new office manager are likely to have some doubts as to whether they can do the job now that they have it.

A changing situation forces us to find new ways of adapt-

The greater the life change and burden of stress, the lower the body's resistance to disease and the more serious the illness that develops.

# THE HOLMES-RAHE LIFE
# EVENT-STRESS SCALE

| Rank | Life event | Mean value |
|---|---|---|
| 1 | Death of spouse | 100 |
| 2 | Divorce | 65 |
| 3 | Marital separation | 65 |
| 4 | Jail term | 63 |
| 5 | Death of close family member | 63 |
| 6 | Personal injury or illness | 53 |
| 7 | Marriage | 50 |
| 8 | Fired at work | 47 |
| 9 | Marital reconciliation | 45 |
| 10 | Retirement | 45 |
| 11 | Change in health of family member | 44 |
| 12 | Pregnancy | 40 |
| 13 | Sex difficulties | 39 |
| 14 | Gain of new family member | 39 |
| 15 | Business readjustment | 39 |
| 16 | Change in financial state | 38 |
| 17 | Death of close friend | 37 |
| 18 | Change to different line of work | 36 |
| 19 | Change in number of arguments with spouse | 35 |
| 20 | Mortgage over $10,000 | 31 |
| 21 | Foreclosure of mortgage or loan | 30 |
| 22 | Change in responsibilities at work | 29 |
| 23 | Son or daughter leaving home | 29 |
| 24 | Trouble with in-laws | 29 |
| 25 | Outstanding personal achievement | 28 |
| 26 | Spouse begins or stops work | 26 |
| 27 | Beginning or ending school | 26 |
| 28 | Change in living condition | 25 |
| 29 | Revision of personal habits | 24 |
| 30 | Trouble with boss | 23 |
| 31 | Change in work hours or conditions | 20 |
| 32 | Change in residence | 20 |
| 33 | Change in schools | 20 |
| 34 | Change in recreation | 19 |
| 35 | Change in church activities | 19 |
| 36 | Change in social activities | 18 |
| 37 | Mortgage or loan less than $10,000 | 17 |
| 38 | Change in sleeping habits | 16 |
| 39 | Change in number of family get-togethers | 15 |
| 40 | Change in eating habits | 15 |
| 41 | Vacation | 13 |
| 42 | Christmas | 12 |
| 43 | Minor violation of the law | 11 |

> # Stress may be associated with positive events such as marriage, promotion, and personal achievement.

ing, and there can be no certainty how well the new ways will work out. There is always a possibility that we will be worse off rather than better off following change.

With change, the status quo is threatened and, no matter how poor it may seem, it provides some degree of security. Change may mean gains, but it also means loss on the psychological level. Whatever the rewards resulting from change, there is still stress because of loss of the old and familiar.

The Holmes-Rahe scale may have several values for you. It indicates the life events that lead to extra stress as perceived by a substantial sample of people. It may help you, if you are feeling stress, to realize why.

It may suggest to you the need, more or less urgent, to develop ways to cope with the stresses in your life more effectively, with much less of the wear and tear and other consequences we will be looking at in Chapters 4 through 7.

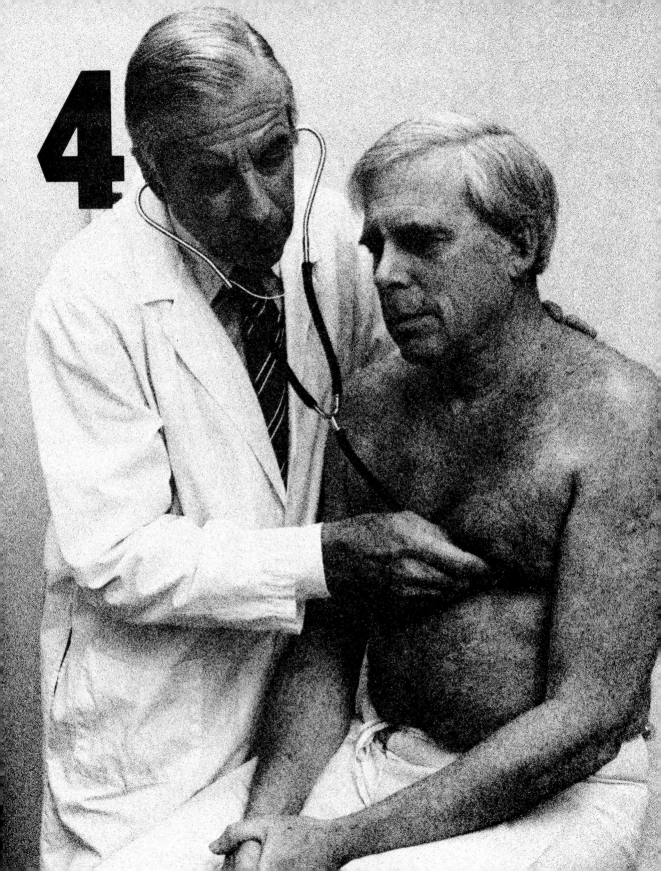

# STRESS
# AND THE HEART

**A**t a recent American Heart Association meeting, Eugene Sprague, M.D., was given an arteriosclerosis research award for young investigators. The brilliant young University of Texas scientist had pointed to a mechanism by which stress is related to atherosclerosis, the artery-clogging disease that leads to heart attacks and strokes.

Sprague had been studying seventy-seven air force pilots, including some with atherosclerosis. He had found that those with evidence of the artery disease also showed aberrant levels of cortisol, the adrenal gland hormone whose release is known to be promoted by stress.

Usually, our cortisol level is highest at about 8 A.M. and then gradually decreases until about 3 P.M., when it begins to rise back to the 8 A.M. level.

But, in the pilots with atherosclerosis, the 8 A.M. levels, although not unusually high, did not decrease as much as did the morning levels of the pilots without significant artery disease. In the latter, cortisol declined from 19 milligrams per deciliter of blood to 8 milligrams between 8 A.M. and 10 A.M., but the levels of pilots with atherosclerosis declined in that time from 20 to 12 milligrams.

To determine whether the change in cortisol concentration could be playing a role in atherosclerosis, Sprague set about reproducing the higher cortisol levels of the atherosclerosis pilots in adult male monkeys. Some of the monkeys were placed on a high-cholesterol diet; others received both a high-cholesterol diet and cortisol.

After a year, the animals were sacrificed and their arteries were examined. Approximately twice as much area was affected by atherosclerosis in arteries from the monkeys getting the combination of high-cholesterol diet and cortisol as in the others.

"I expected to see an increase in atherosclerosis in the monkeys on the high-cholesterol, high-cortisol diet, but I was surprised it was so high," Sprague says.

The Sprague study is only one of the latest indicting stress as a significant promoter of heart disease.

## The Cuckolded Baboons and Other Stressed Creatures

The possible effects of stress on the heart have been investigated in animals as well as humans. We shall come to the humans in the next section.

Animal studies, of course, have advantages. With animals, you can set up constraints, restraints, and other situations not readily achieved with humans.

In one study, the subjects were squirrel monkeys who, for a week, were restrained and subjected, 8 hours on and 8 hours off, to electrical shocks and the stress of working to avoid them. At the end of the week, all showed marked electrocardiographic abnormalities, abnormal heart rhythms, and extensive heart muscle damage.

In another study, this one in the Soviet Union, the subjects were baboons. The male of a particular baboon species, the hamydryas, adopts his females when they are still immature and becomes intensely attached to them. The Russian investigators separated dominant male hamydryas from their females and young. Then, in each case, they put another male in the females' cage in full view of the former consort. The displaced males showed intense agitation, which was hardly unexpected. What the Russian scientists did not expect were the dramatic effects of the stress on the baboons' hearts and circulations. They ended up, after several months, with sixteen baboons with markedly elevated blood pressures, nineteen with coronary insufficiency, and six with heart attacks.

There was also the experience of a certain zoo that found

The artery disease which affects such vessels as those feeding the heart muscle used to be called arteriosclerosis, which means artery hardening. It is now called atherosclerosis; *athero* means soft swelling. And atherosclerosis is a more accurate descriptive term than arteriosclerosis because the disease process starts with a soft swelling and then progresses to hardening.

itself with an alarming increase in deaths in animals and birds from coronary heart disease. Between 1948 and 1968, the heart death rate shot up from less than 1 percent to 10 percent. The diet had not been changed. But over that 20-year period, the zoo had attempted to group the animals socially, and the contrived grouping had led to conflicts, breeding failures, and abnormal behavior.

Investigators had to conclude that the increase in coronary heart disease resulted from behavioral responses to the socially stressful situations. To double-check, in a follow-up study they separated out some animals from a group of swine. At the end of a year, the separated animals, in response to the separation stress, were showing a dramatic rise in both incidence and severity of coronary heart disease.

## Human Heart Attacks and What Precedes Them

Irving S. Wright, M.D., is a distinguished cardiologist who has served as national chairman of the Intersociety Commission for Heart Disease Resources. At a special symposium on stress a few years ago, he made a point of noting that while some skeptics had doubted over the years whether stress could be related to a sudden heart attack, ex-

---

The observation that in humans, the head can influence the heart is hardly new. Almost 2000 years ago, a first-century Roman physician, Celsus, recognized that "fear and anger and any other state of the mind may often be apt to excite the pulse."

In 1628, William Harvey, discoverer of the fact that blood circulates in the body, reaffirmed Celsus's observation by noting that "every affection of the mind that is attended with

either pain or pleasure, hope or fear, is the cause of an agitation whose influence extends to the heart."

Later, the interrelationship between psyche and heart was noted by the great eighteenth-century Scottish physician and physiologist John Hunter, in a self-fulfilling prophecy: "My life is at the mercy of any scoundrel who chooses to put me in a passion."

# THE HEAD AND THE HEART

perienced physicians have seen many examples. He reported:*

> In my own experience, these have occurred many times after business failure, indictment for a crime, death of a spouse—how often a partner of many years dies shortly after the death of the first—anger at a business meeting, and so forth. . . .
>
> Sports events now are recognized as a very common precipitating cause, so much so that mobile coronary care units are increasingly used at race tracks and football stadiums. Their use has been more commonly for the spectators than the athletes. Some patients cannot even tolerate exciting sports events or other stressful shows on television without angina or serious reactions.

Recently, Canadian physicians published a study on the immediate antecedents of heart attacks in 102 active men, between 30 to 60 years of age. On the day of the attack, twenty-four of the men had experienced unusual annoyance; twenty-seven had had to face an unusual business problem; twelve had been bothered by an unusual social or domestic problem; and four had had an unusual financial problem.

Cardiologist Robert S. Eliot, and several colleagues did a study of Cape Kennedy workers who put men on the moon in 1969. The workers were racing to complete their mission, aware that the space budget would be reduced and that they faced the loss of their jobs once a successful moon landing had been completed. The investigators found high rates of divorce and alcohol consumption among these workers. They also noticed an unusual number of sudden deaths, apparently from heart attacks, among the relatively young workers. The deaths ran 50 percent higher than would ordinarily occur among men in that age group.

At the autopsies, the heart muscle was found to show a kind of damage not usually associated with heart attacks. It appeared that the hearts had been thrown into "overdrive" by excessive levels of chemicals that transmit nerve im-

---

* Irving S. Wright, M.D., "Cardiovascular Diseases: Role of Psychogenic and Behavior Patterns in Development and Aggravation," *New York State Journal of Medicine*, October 1975.

pulses. Later, using injections of the same chemicals, Dr. Eliot was able to induce similar heart damage in animals.

More recently, Dr. James E. Skinner and colleagues reported an intriguing observation:*

> Medical researchers have shown that a variety of severe life stresses, among them bereavement, marital troubles, job insecurity, even carrying a large mortgage, are often associated with heart attacks. But they have been unable to describe the exact mechanism that leads to these puzzling cases when an otherwise healthy person suddenly drops dead.
>
> My colleagues and I may now have discovered a missing piece of the puzzle. Recent studies in our laboratory show that heart rhythm and force of contraction are regulated by the frontal cortex of the brain, the same center that mobilizes the body and focuses the sensory receptors when an animal is threatened. Under extra stress, the frontal cortex may—by a process not yet fully understood—send heart muscles into fatal fibrillation [a useless quivering of the heart].

## The Type A Personality

Most commonly, heart attack victims have coronary heart disease caused by atherosclerosis, or the laying down of fatty deposits that narrow the channels of the coronary arteries that feed the heart muscle. Investigators over the years have established a whole series of influences—risk factors —that are likely to bring on the disease: high levels of blood fats, high blood pressure, family history of heart disease, obesity, sedentary living, cigarette smoking.

But not all heart patients have high cholesterol levels; not all are hypertensive; not all have an impressive collection of other risk factors. And even when many such factors are present, there is no certainty that a heart attack will ensue.

Because largely physical factors alone do not provide the complete answer, many researchers have come to consider that stress can be a major influence. And, of late, more and more have been concluding that so-called Type A behavior

* James E. Skinner, M.D., "Heart Attack Trigger," *Psychology Today*, July 1980.

# SELF-EVALUATION: THE GLAZER-STRESSCONTROL LIFE-STYLE QUESTIONNAIRE*

As you can see, each scale below is composed of a pair of adjectives or phrases separated by a series of horizontal lines. Each pair has been chosen to represent two kinds of contrasting behavior. Each of us belongs somewhere along the line between the two extremes. Since most of us are neither the most competitive nor the least competitive person we know, put a check mark where you think you belong between the two extremes.

|  | 1 | 2 | 3 | 4 | 5 | 6 | 7 |  |
|---|---|---|---|---|---|---|---|---|
| 1. Doesn't mind leaving things temporarily unfinished | — | — | — | — | — | — | — | Must get things finished once started |
| 2. Calm and unhurried about appointments | — | — | — | — | — | — | — | Never late for appointments |
| 3. Not competitive | — | — | — | — | — | — | — | Highly competitive |
| 4. Listens well, lets others finish speaking | — | — | — | — | — | — | — | Anticipates others in conversation (nods, interrupts, finishes sentences for the other) |
| 5. Never in a hurry, even when pressured | — | — | — | — | — | — | — | Always in a hurry |
| 6. Able to wait calmly | — | — | — | — | — | — | — | Uneasy when waiting |
| 7. Easygoing | — | — | — | — | — | — | — | Always going full speed ahead |
| 8. Takes one thing at a time | — | — | — | — | — | — | — | Tries to do more than one thing at a time, thinks about what to do next |
| 9. Slow and deliberate in speech | — | — | — | — | — | — | — | Vigorous and forceful in speech (uses a lot of gestures) |
| 10. Concerned with satisfying himself, not others | — | — | — | — | — | — | — | Wants recognition by others for a job well done |
| 11. Slow doing things | — | — | — | — | — | — | — | Fast doing things (eating, walking, etc.) |
| 12. Easygoing | — | — | — | — | — | — | — | Hard driving |
| 13. Expresses feelings openly | — | — | — | — | — | — | — | Holds feelings in |
| 14. Has a large number of interests | — | — | — | — | — | — | — | Few interests outside work |
| 15. Satisfied with job | — | — | — | — | — | — | — | Ambitious, wants quick advancement on job |

|   | 1 | 2 | 3 | 4 | 5 | 6 | 7 |   |
|---|---|---|---|---|---|---|---|---|
| 16. Never sets own deadlines | — | — | — | — | — | — | — | Often sets own deadlines |
| 17. Feels limited responsibility | — | — | — | — | — | — | — | Always feels responsible |
| 18. Never judges things in terms of numbers | — | — | — | — | — | — | — | Often judges performance in terms of numbers (how many, how much) |
| 19. Casual about work | — | — | — | — | — | — | — | Takes work very seriously (works weekends, brings work home) |
| 20. Not very precise | — | — | — | — | — | — | — | Very precise (careful about detail) |

SCORING: Assign a value from 1 to 7 for each score. Total them up. The categories are as follows:

Total score = 110 – 140: Type $A_1$.

If you are in this category, and especially if you are over 40 and smoke, you are likely to have a high risk of developing cardiac illness.

Total score = 80 – 109: Type $A_2$.

You are in the direction of being cardiac prone, but your risk is not as high as the $A_1$. You should, nevertheless, pay careful attention to the advice given to all Type A's.

Total score = 60 – 79: Type AB.

You are an admixture of A and B patterns. This is a healthier pattern than either $A_1$ or $A_2$, but you have the potential for slipping into A behavior and you should recognize this.

Total score = 30 – 59: Type $B_2$.

Your behavior is on the less-cardiac-prone end of the spectrum. You are generally relaxed and cope adequately with stress.

Total score = 0 – 29: Type $B_1$.

You tend to the extreme of non-cardiac traits. Your behavior expresses few of the reactions associated with cardiac disease.

This test will give you some idea of where you stand in the discussion of Type A behavior that follows. The higher your score, the more cardiac prone you tend to be. Remember, though, even B persons occasionally slip into A behavior, and any of these patterns can change over time.

* This questionnaire was designed by Dr. Howard I. Glazer, director of behavior management systems at EHE Stresscontrol Systems, Inc.

is a prime candidate as a major psychological cause of heart attacks. In a nutshell, those who exhibit Type A behavior live under nearly constant stress, and much of that stress is self-imposed.

Although the connection between the A behavior pattern and coronary heart disease was first proposed in 1959, almost two decades passed before it received any general acceptance. In December 1978, a panel of twenty-five distinguished cardiologists, epidemiologists, and psychologists met under the auspices of the National Heart, Lung and Blood Institute of the National Institutes of Health to review the available data on Type A behavior. They concluded that it was indeed a serious risk factor for coronary heart disease.

One possible reason for the delay has been recently noted by one of the originators of the Type A concept, Meyer Friedman, M.D., who has observed:

> We were taking what is widely believed to be just the sort of behavior and personality necessary for successful living in Western society and calling it a disorder. And many of our fellow cardiologists themselves suffered quite severely from this same Type A behavior.

### The Clues

More than 40 years ago, Drs. Karl and William Menninger of the Menninger Clinic were among the first psychiatrists to become interested in studying the personalities of patients suffering from coronary heart disease. They noted that many such patients appeared to be aggressive—but under the surface.

A decade later, another psychiatrist, Flanders Dunbar,

Those who exhibit Type A behavior live under nearly constant stress, and much of that stress is self-imposed.

examined a large group of coronary patients and found them to be hard-driving individuals with single-direction personalities seeking refuge in work. She also concluded that they had less interest in sports, more illnesses, and less sexual tranquility than noncoronary subjects.

Almost at the same time, another distinguished psychiatrist, J. A. Arlow, found that these coronary patients seemed to share a secret insecurity, a belief that they were shams. Because their real accomplishments failed to assuage that belief, they had an incessant need to go after new successes.

But it remained for Dr. Friedman and his colleague, Ray H. Rosenman, M.D., to establish, much later, an impressive case for the importance of personality and behavior in coronary heart disease.

## The Pattern

The two San Francisco physicians described two major types of personality, A and B, with A being coronary-prone.

"If an individual with behavior pattern A were forced to display or wear a heraldic emblem consonant with his personality," Friedman has written, "a most appropriate symbol might well be a clenched fist holding a stopwatch."

Type A persons are aggressive, ambitious, highly competitive; they have intense drive; they must get things done; and they make a habit of pitting themselves against the clock. On the other hand, a B person may be just as serious but is much more easygoing, able to enjoy leisure, and with no feelings of being driven by time. Most of us are mixtures, with characteristics of both types, usually one or the other being predominant in varying degrees.

Typically, Type A persons are briskly self-confident, decisive, never dawdling. In speech, they tend to use various words of their sentences as battering rams. They have a compulsion to overwork and often neglect other aspects of their lives, such as family, social events, leisure, and recreational activities.

Typically, too, they are aggressive with hostile feelings. Playing games, even with their children, they play to win. They love competing with fellow workers and would much

# "THE CHRONIC AND INCESSANT STRUGGLE"

Some new insights into the Type A pattern have come from Dr. Friedman, writing in *The Sciences,* a publication of the New York Academy of Sciences:*

"The Type A behavior pattern is an action-emotion complex exhibited by people who are unable—or unwilling—to evaluate their own competence. Such people prefer to judge themselves by the evaluations of those whom they believe are their superiors. And to enhance themselves in other people's eyes, they attempt to increase the quantity (but rarely the quality) of their achievements. Their self-esteem becomes increasingly dependent on the status they believe they achieve.

"Unfortunately, such people pay a price. Any degree of self-esteem which they gain in this manner is apparently not enough to allay the insecurity and consequent agitation engendered by their 'surrender' to outside criteria, to the authority of others.

"Hoping, nevertheless, to achieve a satisfactory sense of self-esteem, such people incessantly try to increase the sheer quantity of their achievements. And it is this chronic and incessant struggle to achieve more and more in less time, together with a free-floating but covert, and usually well-rationalized, hostility, that make up the Type A behavior pattern. The sense of urgency and hostility give rise to irritation, impatience, aggravation, and anger; the four components which I believe comprise the pathogenetic core of the behavior pattern."

* Meyer Friedman, M.D., "Type A Behavior: A Progress Report," *The Sciences,* February 1980.

rather have the respect than the affection of their associates. Conscious always of time, they have a great need to try to get more and more done in a given period. They are punctual, unable to tolerate waiting even briefly for a table in a restaurant. If a person's mate has advised slowing down, chances are good that the person is a Type A, observes Dr. Friedman.

Executives with Type A personality often have no inkling that the pressures they are under may come from within themselves rather than from external circumstances.

At one recent seminar on handling stress, one executive remarked: "I always have the feeling that nobody can do this but me!" Whereupon many of the other executive participants smiled in appreciation and acknowledged: "That's exactly how I feel."

## The Testing

In 1955, Drs. Friedman and Rosenman became distinctly impressed by the presence of certain traits, later to be identified as indicative of Type A behavior, in almost every one of their middle-aged and younger coronary patients. They were traits not seen nearly so often in patients with noncardiac disorders.

Friedman and Rosenman proceeded to do a simple thing that brought a jolting response. They questioned some 200 business executives and about 75 physicians who were treating heart patients. What, in their opinion, caused heart attacks in friends and patients? Three-fourths of both the doctors and the executives incriminated the same things: excessive drive and deadline-meeting.

Friedman and Rosenman then asked a group of laypersons to select from among friends and associates those who seemed most obviously to have a pattern of Type A behavior. The names of eighty-three men were furnished. Union executives then were asked to choose, from among members of their organizations, eighty-three individuals who exhibited most obviously just the opposite behavior pattern, Type B. In addition, the investigators studied forty-six blind men who manifested chronic anxiety and insecurity.

The dietary intake of total calories, total fats, and animal fats was investigated and found to be essentially the same for all three groups, as was the amount of physical activity. Blood and electrocardiographic studies were made.

The findings: 23 of the 83 Type A men (28 percent) showed evidence of coronary heart disease, while only 3 of the Type B men (4 percent) and 2 of the 46 anxiety cases suffered from the disease. Thus, Type A men had 7 times as much coronary heart disease as Type B men.

Those figures do not mean that any large group of Type A people will have 7 times as much disease as a large group of Type B's. For, in this study, most of the Type A and most of the Type B persons chosen as obviously "typical" were of the fully developed or extreme type. The researchers later found a much lower proportion of the fully developed cases in large, unselected groups. But the results do suggest that subjects with Type A behavior are relatively prone, and those with Type B are relatively immune, to early occurrences of coronary heart disease.

Women were also studied: 125 with Type A and 132 with Type B behavior, all chosen by lay people. Most of the A's worked in industry or the professions; most of the B's were primarily homemakers. The A women turned out to have almost 5 times as much coronary heart disease as the B women.

But, while such studies indicated that among people selected from a general population, those with fully developed A behavior had much more coronary heart disease than those with B, they did not prove that people with Type A but without existing heart disease would develop the disease in the future more frequently than individuals with Type B.

So, in 1960 and 1961, the Western Collaborative Study Group was organized, enlisting more than 3500 men, aged 39 to 59, apparently free of heart disease. For each man, a careful history was obtained along with detailed information on diet; drinking and smoking habits; measurements of blood pressure, blood fats, and other factors; plus an assessment of behavior pattern.

Four years later, 52 of the 3500 men had developed their first heart attack and 18 their first attack of anginal chest pain associated with coronary heart disease. The dietary intake and other factors had been much the same for those who became ill and for the group as a whole. But the incidence of coronary heart disease proved to be 3 times as great in the group originally classified as showing Type A behavior as in those believed to be Type B.

## Interplay: Type A, Stress, and Heart Attack

For years, working at the University of Texas, Dr. David C. Glass, a psychologist, has focused his research on the interplay between Type A personality, life stress, and heart attack.

As he has noted, stress can make a heart attack more likely by increasing levels of cholesterol in the bloodstream. Also, it can cause the same result by increasing blood pres-

# The Type A women turned out to have almost five times as much coronary heart disease as the B women.

sure so that blood passing through the arteries under high pressure increases the likelihood of tears in the arterial walls, around which fatty deposits can form. Further, stress can cause release of hormones which, in the process of mobilizing the body to cope with danger, speed up blood clotting, increasing the likelihood that a vessel-blocking blood clot may form.

For all these reasons, Glass reports, stress makes the danger of heart attack more likely. And for the person with Type A behavior, the risk is even greater.

In his own laboratory, Glass has found high cholesterol levels in extreme Type A men as young as 19 years of age. He has also determined that in Type A men, blood pressure increases sharply when hostility is aroused. Moreover, the blood-clotting time of Type A is significantly faster than that of others and, Glass notes, some evidence indicates that they react to stress with greater hormone secretion.

Glass has also found that in Type A's, the push to achieve leads them to press their bodies to the limit. He asked subjects to walk continuously on a motorized treadmill at increasingly sharp angles of incline until they gave up. Every few minutes, as they walked on the treadmill, they rated their level of fatigue. Glass then measured the subjects' aerobic capacity individually to see how close they had pushed themselves to their lungs' capacity to absorb oxygen.

Type A subjects reached 91.5 percent of capacity; Type Bs, only 82.8 percent. "Even so," says Glass, "As admitted to less fatigue than Bs did. The hard-driving As ignore or deny their body's tiredness in their struggle to attain their goals— in this case, a superior performance on a treadmill."

As Glass sees it, Type A persons have to master challenges out of a need to control their world, and the concept

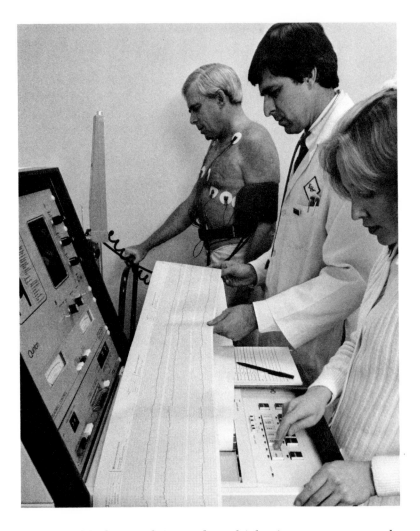

of control helps explain under which circumstances such persons are more vulnerable to heart attack. Given concern about controlling the environment, a Type A person should be upset by threats to that control, and even more distressed when a threat is beyond the person's control so that,

## Stress makes the danger of heart attack more likely.

regardless of effort, he or she can do nothing to master the situation.

In one study, Glass compared a group of men aged 35 to 55 hospitalized for heart attack with a group hospitalized for other kinds of disease and with healthy, nonhospitalized men. The heart attack victims had stronger Type A patterns than either of the other two groups. But Glass comments:[*]

> Of greater interest, though, were their scores on a Loss Index, a 10-item scale that asks a person to describe the incidence during the last year of stressful events in his life over which he had minimal control, such as a loved one's death, being fired, or a significant financial loss. Within the year preceding their illness, both hospitalized groups experienced more such losses than had the healthy group. Life events that leave a person feeling bereft and helpless can lead to disease. In the face of uncontrollable losses, a Type A person is likely to have a heart attack, while one lower in Type A traits will more often develop some other disease.

In one experiment, Glass exposed Type A and Type B subjects to bursts of very loud noise. In the first session, half of them could escape by mastering a tricky pattern of lever pressing; half could do nothing to escape the noise. In the second session, everyone had a chance to learn to escape.

After the sessions, Glass found, those who were unable to escape reported that they felt quite helpless. In fact, some who had been in the session where escape was impossible sat dejectedly through the second session when they could have escaped, listening passively to the noisy bursts without lifting a hand. Most of the helpless people were Type A's; being unable to escape hit them especially hard. Once frustrated by unavoidable noise, those Type A's who did escape took much longer to learn to shut off the noise, while the B's performed equally well whether or not they had been frustrated. Glass has concluded:

> These complicated reactions seem to indicate that the Type A person at first rises to any challenge. He tries hard to control a highly stressful situation, but when his best efforts fail, he feels helpless and his attempts to master it suffer. The death of someone close, the loss of a job, or a financial setback are all

[*] David C. Glass, "Stress, Competition, and Heart Attacks," *Psychology Today*, December 1976.

# Although life's tragedies are hard for anyone, they are particularly dangerous for the Type A person.

events that we can do little to remedy. Although life's tragedies are hard for anyone, they are particularly dangerous for the Type A person. For him, they can spell heart attack—and even death.

## Sudden Death

That stress may produce sudden death is no new idea. Since biblical times, instances have been noted of the apparently sudden deaths of people while gripped by rage, fear, humiliation, and even joy.

Is there any scientific foundation for the idea? Many animal studies have strongly associated psychological stress with abnormal and fatal heart rhythms. Moreover, the most effective way of inducing such stress and its fatal consequences has been to subject animals to situations beyond their control.

It is difficult, of course, to conduct controlled studies with humans to establish a relationship between stress and sudden death. But there have been instances in which electrocardiographic monitoring of the hearts of humans performing stressful tasks has shown serious, even potentially fatal, rhythm disturbances.

For example, investigators have reported the case of a 38-year-old man with conflicts about his work who was studied 6 weeks after a heart attack. During an hour-long interview, his heart rhythm was continuously monitored while his facial expressions were filmed. As judged from the filmed interview, periods of stress correlated well with the appearance and frequency of abnormal rhythms. During treadmill-exercise stress testing, however, very few such rhythms developed, suggesting that the man's heart was more sensitive to emotional than to physical stress.

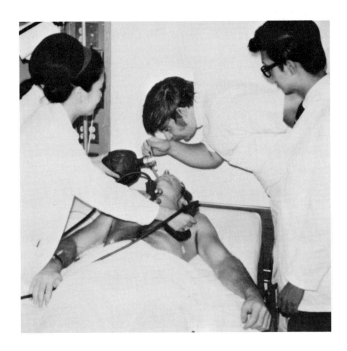

In one investigation, Bernard Lown, M.D., and other Harvard University School of Public Health researchers closely evaluated 117 patients with often-recurring, life-threatening abnormal rhythms in their psychological, emotional, and physical activities. In a number of these patients, three sets of conditions contributing to dangerous rhythm appeared to be operating. The first was the presence of some electrical instability of the heart muscle, usually associated with coronary heart disease. The second was the presence of a psychological state of some intensity—either mental depression or a sense of being psychologically trapped without possible exit. The third condition was a psychological trigger, an emotional stress that occurred within 24 hours before onset of abnormal rhythm.

Lown and his colleagues identified 25 patients in particular who were different from the other 92 in having less demonstrable physical heart problems while experiencing more serious rhythm abnormalities. In 15 of the 25, the psychological triggering event occurred less than an hour before onset of the rhythm abnormality. The most common stress, in 17 of the 25, was anger.

There have been other significant studies as well. Some years ago, researchers investigated a then remarkable community in Pennsylvania, Roseto, where rural people of Italian descent consumed a diet very high in fats and cholesterol, yet had a very low death rate from heart attacks. The families were closely knit and stable. But more recently, with increasing urbanization, disruption of family units, and growing stress, the sudden-death rate of Roseto has risen markedly and is approaching the rates of nearby communities.

Several studies have shown the correlation between recent bereavement and sudden death, especially among men. In one study, the mortality rate for widowers in the year following bereavement was 12.2 percent, compared with 1.2 percent in a matched group of married men of similar age and background.

It has been noted, too, that among patients recovering from heart attacks, sudden deaths occur significantly more often in conjunction with rounds by the chief surgeon than at other times. These deaths, according to investigators, are provoked by the patient's excitement, anxiety, and sometimes disappointment in relation to his or her progress and prospects for quick discharge from the hospital.

In one dramatic case, a young girl suffered her first serious abnormal heart rhythm when she was awakened by a thunderclap. Thereafter, she had repeated episodes of abnormal rhythm whenever she was awakened by an alarm clock.

Another case, reported by Dr. Lown and his colleagues, was that of a 39-year-old man who experienced potentially fatal abnormal rhythm on two occasions, in both of which his heart actually stopped beating.

The first episode occurred when he was roughhousing with his sexually mature teenage daughters. When a neighbor rang the doorbell, he looked up, said, "I'm sorry," and abruptly went into grave rhythm abnormality and heart arrest.

After his successful resuscitation, he was thoroughly studied. He had no structural heart disease. Extensive psychological studies followed during which he was covertly hostile and denied being angry or depressed. Yet, his whole lifestyle pattern was one of controlled aggression. Although he professed an aversion to violence and repressed sexuality, they often were the subjects of his dreams. During some of the psychological interviews, he developed lesser rhythm abnormalities although he was outwardly calm and controlled.

After a second heart stoppage, he was taught to meditate, and he found that during periods of meditation he could suppress abnormal rhythms successfully. He remained well thereafter.

## Hypertension

During a great oil fire in Texas, a major earthquake in Iran, and the Germans' siege of Leningrad in World War II, the incidence of hypertension—high blood pressure—was found to have increased by as much as 300 percent.

The increase is no surprise. The ability of stress to raise blood pressure is well documented. Undoubtedly you know this fact from your own experience. When your physician takes your blood pressure during a routine checkup, you have probably noticed that the procedure is done more than once. You are under some stress, especially at the beginning of the checkup, from just being examined. So the first pressure measurement is likely to be higher than another measurement taken later after you have become a little more relaxed.

Hypertension is a major threat to health, contributing significantly as it does to heart attacks and, as well, to strokes and kidney failure. It ranks as our greatest single cause of death.

# The ability of stress to raise blood pressure is well documented.

# Hypertension ranks as our greatest single cause of death.

## The Normal and the High Pressures

Blood pressure is the force exerted against artery walls as blood flows through the blood vessels. The pressure is produced primarily by the pumping action of the heart and is needed to push the body's 5 quarts of blood through more than 60,000 miles of blood vessels.

Each time the heart beats, pressure increases. This higher pressure is known as the *systolic* pressure (systolic, from the Greek word for contraction). The pressure is at its lowest when the heart relaxes between beats. This is known as the *diastolic* pressure (from the Greek word for expansion).

Normal systolic pressure at rest is in the range of 100 to 140, and normal diastolic pressure is 60 to 90. A blood pressure reading is expressed by both figures, with systolic over diastolic: 140/90, for example. Because blood pressure varies normally under different circumstances, a single reading above 140/90 does not indicate abnormal pressure. But when the pressure is continuously elevated, hypertension is present.

### The Silent Killer

Hypertension is stealthy, readily detected by a physician taking measurements, but otherwise not likely to be apparent to the victim. Mild elevations, and often severe ones also, commonly produce no symptoms at all for long periods. The symptoms, including headaches, dizziness, fatigue, weakness, are common to many disorders. So, even when they do appear, they may not be recognized as related to elevated pressure.

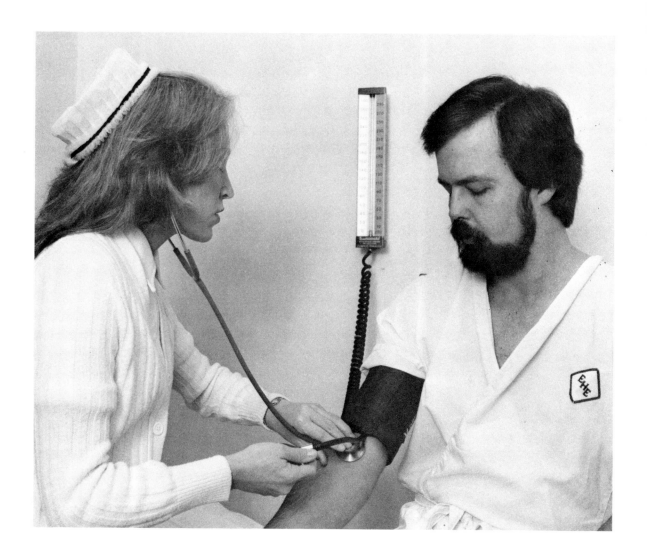

But, even though producing no symptoms, elevated pressure over long periods can have serious effects. It requires the heart to work harder to pump blood. So the heart muscle thickens and increases in size as a consequence. For a time, despite its increased work, the heart accommodates well. But at some point it can become fatigued, no longer fully able to meet the strain. The result may be congestive heart failure—reduced blood circulation to body tissues—which can lead to such symptoms as loss of energy, shortness of breath on exertion, wheezing, and fluid accumulation in body tissues.

Hypertension may have another effect on the heart. As the heart muscle increases in size, the coronary arteries supplying it do not. They have spare capacity, and that may be enough. But, in some cases, it may not be. Coronary insufficiency may then develop, with resulting chest pain (angina pectoris).

Persistent hypertension can reduce blood supply to the kidneys, impairing their function, sometimes leading to complete kidney failure and uremic poisoning and death. High pressure may also lead to rupture, or blowout, of a brain artery—in other words, a stroke.

Moreover, recent research has been assigning a critical role for hypertension in atherosclerosis. Other factors, of course, play a part: obesity, high blood-fat levels, cigarette smoking, sedentary living. But many studies have shown that a very large proportion of people who experience heart attacks, the end result of atherosclerosis of the coronary arteries of the heart, have elevated pressure. On the other hand, in the federal government's long-term study in Framingham, which for many years has been following more than 5000 people in that Massachusetts community, men and women with normal blood pressure have experienced only one-fourth the rate of coronary heart disease generally found among people of their age and sex.

How does hypertension foster atherosclerosis? One possible way is by the abnormal pounding that excessive pressure exerts on the inner linings of arteries. This pounding is severe enough, some investigators believe, to damage the lining surfaces and open the way for the fatty, clogging deposits to be laid down.

Recent research has been assigning a critical role for hypertension in atherosclerosis.

## Causes

High blood pressure can be the result of kidney disease. Some cases stem from tumors, often benign, of the adrenal glands. But in 90 percent, or even more, of all cases of hypertension, there is no such organic cause and the hypertension is called "essential" or "primary," that is, of unknown cause.

But, even though exact causes are unknown, certain predisposing factors have been established.

Heredity is one. If, for example, one of your parents is hypertensive, chances that you will develop the disease are 2 to 3 times greater than for the general population.

Obesity is another factor. Studies have shown that among men and women over 35, the incidence of hypertension averages twice as high in the obese as in the normal population. Also, clinical studies have found that blood pressure commonly declines when excess weight is lost.

Excess salt in the diet is still another significant factor. Studies have shown that primitive tribes, for example, without salt in their diet suffer no hypertension. Even at age 60, men of one Brazilian Indian tribe have been found to have blood pressures averaging 100/60.

## Stress as Culprit

Many studies have demonstrated the marked effect of stress on blood pressure.

For example, using equipment that could monitor blood pressure continuously, investigators checked on the reactions of a pilot who was about to make a test flight. At the last minute, a mechanical difficulty in the test plane was discovered. For 4 hours, he waited while technicians corrected the problem. In that time, as he became more and more impatient and frustrated, his blood pressure went up and up. Once the difficulty was fixed and he could get on with the job, his blood pressure dropped.

Researchers have monitored blood pressures of several dozen men whose jobs were threatened. They checked pressures for each man while he was anticipating loss of his job, as soon as he knew he had lost it, during the time he was out of work, during trial reemployment, and finally, when he had a regular job again.

They found that pressures stayed high all through the period of stress, which lasted from the time of threatened job loss right through to the time when regular work could be resumed; only when the men felt secure once more did pressure drop.

In experiments at Michael Reese Hospital, Chicago, persons with normal blood pressure were deliberately exposed to anger-provoking situations. In those who bottled up their anger, blood pressure shot up; in those who freely vented their anger, there was less elevation.

In a wide variety of laboratory situations of emotional stress, investigators have been able to document the effects on blood pressure. They have found, for example, that among people who already have some degree of elevation, interviews about personal histories and current life situations produced further pressure increases of as much as 40 points and more. There were variations among subjects and from one moment to another in the same subject; the changes were closely related to the degree to which a subject got emotionally involved with the interviewer and the topics under discussion.

To extend such studies to longer periods of observation and to natural life situations, researchers developed a portable blood pressure recorder. Thus, subjects could record their pressures on a preset schedule, usually every half-hour, as they went about ordinary activities outside the laboratory.

The subjects also kept logs of their activities, checking a list of adjectives describing moods or attitudes after each pressure measurement: anxiety, hostility, depression, feel-

. . . blood pressure commonly declines when excess weight is lost.

# Their bodies get used to responding to daily life as if to a series of emergencies.

ings of time pressure (all negative effects), and alertness and contentment (positive effects). Consistently, blood pressures were markedly higher whenever negative effects were reported in the logs.

A group of male executives were studied for 2 days through their usual workdays and into the evenings. Under emotional stress, the pressure for the average man increased by about 50 points and in some cases by more than 80.

As the American Heart Association has pointed out:

> Wrapped up somehow in the whole business of high blood pressure is the subject of emotion. When a person is angry or afraid, his blood pressure may go up. It may increase just because he knows he is going to have his blood pressure taken. Rises like these, during times of stress, are perfectly normal.
>
> But some individuals react to even mild life stresses with an excessive rise in blood pressure. (When the stress has passed, the blood pressure returns to normal.) These men and women are called hyper-reactors or pre-hypertensives. Chances are that in time many of them will develop hypertension. Their bodies simply get used to responding to daily life as if it were a series of emergencies.

The significance of stress in hypertension is highlighted by the fact, too, that while drugs are effective in lowering elevated pressure, in many cases such stress-reducing techniques as biofeedback and meditation reduce the quantity of drugs needed or even eliminate any need for them.

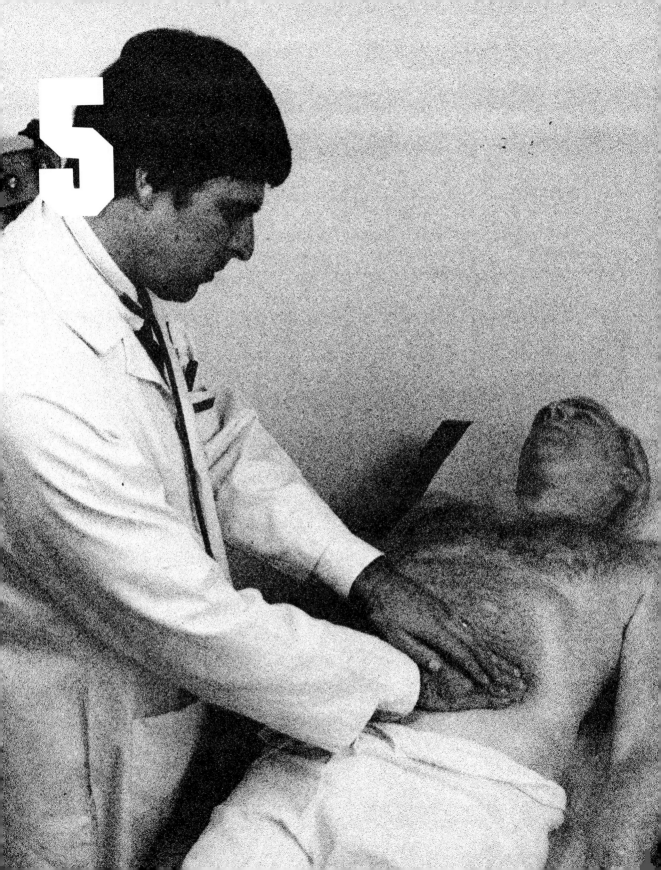

# STRESS AND THE GUT

It's the most common consequence of stress we see at Executive Health Examiners: gut trouble.

It can mean anything from repeated episodes of heartburn, bloating, and a feeling that the digestive system just is not functioning properly to what is often called the "executive wound stripe," the peptic ulcer. Even more often, it is that disconcerting, often confusing collection of afflictions known variously as the "irritable bowel syndrome," "irritable colon," and the "nervous" or "spastic" gut.

No wonder! Virtually everyone responds to stress with some form of physical reaction and no part of the body is more vulnerable than the gastrointestinal tract or gut. The brain is connected to the muscles of the gut by a network of nerves.

Get emotionally upset and you may actually feel your gut muscles tighten and contract in spasms. And a lot more may be going on, in reaction to stress, to make you at the very least, uncomfortable and, at worst, anxious over the possibility of your having a malignant or other potentially serious disease.

## A Serendipitous Look at a Stressed Stomach

Happily, indeed, for science if not for the victim, a shotgun was accidentally discharged in a trader's store in Canada more than a century and a half ago, in June 1822. It provided some of the first real insights into the brain-and-gut connection. The victim was Alexis St. Martin and the shotgun blast tore skin and muscle from the upper part of his abdomen and, in addition, from the outer layer of the wall of his stomach. On being called to help, the best that Dr. William Beaumont, a young United States Army surgeon, could do was to stitch the stomach edges to the skin.

St. Martin lived—with a hole in his stomach. Beaumont, with St. Martin's cooperation, could look in and see the stomach move. He could also see digestive juices oozing onto the stomach lining. He could lower into the stomach a piece of meat on a string, pull it out half an hour later and see a bit of fraying at the meat edges, insert it again for another half-hour and pull it out to find half the meat gone, and reinsert it for another hour, whereupon it was completely dissolved and gone.

With the aid of the peephole in St. Martin's stomach, Beaumont was able to discover that gastric juice appeared only when food was being chewed or when it entered the stomach. And when he sucked up some pure juice through a rubber tube, it proved to be hydrochloric acid.

Beaumont made other observations, including, notably, that St. Martin's stomach underwent marked changes in appearance when he was angry or excited.

About a century later, Dr. Anton Carlson, often called the grand old man of American physiology, also could make some important observations with the aid of a man who, because of a severe burn of the esophagus, had to be fed through a surgical opening in his stomach.

Measuring the amount of gastric juice flowing under various circumstances, Carlson found that it was copious when the man smelled something he liked to eat but dried up when he saw or smelled something unappetizing. (This fact may be why the culinary art is so highly valued; everything else being equal, you are likely to digest a dish you like better than one you do not. And you will probably digest better, too, when circumstances are pleasant rather than otherwise.)

An even more rewarding case was that of Tom Little when he first appeared at New York Hospital in Manhattan in 1941. As a child, Tom had swallowed steaming-hot clam chowder which burned and blocked his esophagus, making it useless. He required surgery to provide an artificial, external opening into his stomach. At the age of 9, he learned to chew his food, remove it from his mouth, and introduce it into a funnel attached to a rubber tube leading to his stom-

> # You will probably digest a dish you like better than one you do not.

ach. Later, he married, and only his family and close friends knew about his injury; he never ate with others.

Then, one day in New York, while doing physical labor, Tom began to bleed from the stomach opening. Apparently his movements at work had irritated the area. He had to be hospitalized, and while he was recovering in the hospital, two medical researchers, Drs. Stewart Wolf and Harold Wolff, then investigating the effects of emotions on the body, persuaded him to be a subject for the study.

The two researchers noted that when Tom became resentful or angry, his stomach changed, much as if it were about to receive a meal, its pink color becoming red and its juices flowing freely. When food was introduced, it would be out of his stomach in less time than usual because of the excessive gastric juice flow.

On the other hand, when he was sad, fearful or depressed, the stomach lining became pale, secretions decreased, and, when depression was severe enough, even introduction of food made no difference. The stomach remained pale and juice flow was restricted. When food was introduced while he was depressed, it might remain in the stomach, undigested, for many hours.

Unpleasant consequences can arise from such emotionally induced effects on the stomach. For example, excessive acidity, when stimulated by anger or other emotions, may aggravate or even possibly induce a peptic ulcer. If some of the excess acid is carried with a gas bubble back from the stomach and up into the esophagus, there can be heartburn.

Nor are the consequences of emotional disturbances limited to the stomach. Anger, resentment, anxiety, humiliation, and feelings of being in overwhelming situations can increase mucus and other secretions in the intestines and increase contractions and other activities there, producing diarrhea and other discomfort. Depression, fear, dejection, feelings of futility or defeat can have the opposite effects, producing constipation and other disturbances.

Popular speech, of course, is full of examples of the intimate connection between feelings and the gut, all suggesting that the gastrointestinal system is commonly regarded as a kind of barometer of stress: "I'm fed up," "I can't swallow that story," "I can't stomach it," and "What's eating you?"

## Behind Indigestion

It goes by many names: dyspepsia, upset stomach, nervous indigestion, acid indigestion, acute indigestion, or just plain indigestion. Few of us escape an occasional experience.

It can sometimes produce midriff discomfort, or, sometimes, upper abdominal pain and distention, gas, belching, nausea, and heartburn singly or in combination.

Stress, of course, is not the only cause.

Possible triggers include gallbladder or liver disease, kidney stones, peptic ulcer, appendicitis, intestinal obstruction, food poisoning, or milk or other food intolerance.

For some people, eating food with high fat content, partaking liberally of such foods as cucumbers, beans, radishes, cabbage, turnips, or onions or such seasonings as garlic, chili, or pepper can produce it.

Normally, stomach motility or food-churning and food-mixing activity is stimulated when the stomach is only moderately full. With overeating, the activity is inhibited, causing sensations of fullness and nausea. Foods high in fat or fried in fat also tend to slow stomach activity and prolong the

# An excess of fatty food can have the same effect as overeating.

stomach's emptying time. Thus, an excess of fatty food can have the same effect as overeating.

Stress can enter the picture in the same way, and in other ways as well. Fear, shock, depression, or other emotional upset tends to slow stomach activity. Eating during an emotional upset may involve eating too rapidly, chewing inadequately, and swallowing a lot of air.

Rapid eating and inadequate chewing of food can prod the stomach into secreting more acid to aid digestion of the food chunks. The additional acid, combined with excessive air swallowed during hurried chewing and swallowing, can irritate the stomach lining.

Mild indigestion often will disappear if you do nothing more than not eat for a few hours. Some relief, too, can be obtained by lying down on the right side, a position that puts gravity to work to help the stomach move its contents along to the small intestine. Antacids, although certainly not essential, may help to provide relief.

When indigestion is severe or occurs frequently or chronically, medical advice is needed. The possibility of organic disease has to be considered. But when such disease is exonerated, the likelihood, for a busy executive under stress, is that stress is the culprit and that the solution to the problem lies in better means of coping.

P.D. is a man who learned how to cope with the stress that caused his ulcer. A 43-year-old advertising executive in the creative department of a large, successful, and very competitive agency, he is known as an extremely talented employee with a penchant for long hours and late nights at work — a very goal-oriented Type A individual. He has been a one- to two-pack-a-day smoker for over 20 years, and his smoking increases in response to stress. He also consumes 10 to 12 cups of coffee a day and, for the past three or four years, has noted, with gradually increasing frequency, symptoms of upper gastrointestinal distress such as indigestion and heartburn. P.D. attributed this discomfort to a "nervous stomach" such as his father had, and he ignored his wife's warning to "slow down a bit." He began taking frequent doses of an over-the-counter antacid, to alleviate his symptoms.

Finally, as his complaints to family and colleagues in-

# Eating during an emotional upset may involve eating too rapidly, chewing inadequately, and swallowing a lot of air.

creased, he was urged to have a "complete physical" at Executive Health Examiners. Careful questioning by the doctor raised the suspicion of ulcer disease. This possible diagnosis was subsequently confirmed by radiographic studies of his gastrointestinal (GI) tract, which revealed an early duodenal ulcer. The doctor emphasized to P.D. that this condition could not be effectively treated unless he modified his lifestyle and cut his tobacco and caffeine intake. Through a combination of self-help relaxation and behavioral modification techniques, the patient was able to decrease his cigarette consumption to half a pack a day and coffee to 2 cups a day; the ulcer healed in 6 weeks on standard medical treatment. Although P.D. continues to work hard, he realizes that

he can no longer push himself beyond his threshold without jeopardizing his health. He continues to modify some of his Type A characteristics under the guidance of an EHE psychologist, and now takes regular vacations and engages in frequent recreational activities.

## The Irritable Bowel: Common "Nervous" Gut

It *is* extremely common—so common that as many as half of all the people with abdominal complaints have it, and some estimates go as high as 60 percent.

It is *not* just a matter of abdominal pain alone or constipation alone.

Its symptoms can be highly variable. There may be abdominal distention; sharp, knifelike or deep, dull abdominal pain; cramps that may mimic those of appendicitis when they occur on the right side (but they sometimes occur on the left).

Frequently, victims suffer from constipation, sometimes alternating with diarrhea. Sometimes, stools appear pencil-like. Some victims see "pus" or "worms" in the stools; they are, in fact, large amounts of mucus.

Many victims complain of lack of appetite in the morning, nausea, heartburn, or excessive belching and, not uncommonly, of weakness, palpitation, headaches, sleeping trouble, faintness, and excessive perspiration.

Life-threatening? Not at all. The condition never leads to cancer and very rarely to any serious complications. But the symptoms can be distressing.

The irritable bowel syndrome comes down to a disturbed state of intestinal motility—with no anatomic cause.

### The Disturbed Balance

An abnormality in the behavior or function of an organ or part of the body in the absence of organic disease is known as a *functional disorder*.

The colon (also called the large intestine or large bowel)

consists of the last 5 feet of the digestive tract. Its main function is to conduct indigestible portions of food or waste material out of the body. Any disruption of this function can lead to symptoms. But it does not mean that the colon is damaged or diseased.

Colon activities are controlled by the nervous system. There are impulses that stimulate activity; others that inhibit it. A fine balance between the two types allows gastrointestinal contents to pass smoothly.

In the irritable colon, the balance is disturbed. Constipation occurs when regular colon contractions are inhibited; diarrhea appears when the contractions are excessive. Abdominal pain and other symptoms may result from spasm of the colon and gas distention of the bowel.

## A Stress Factor

Although knowledge of why the colon malfunctions in the absence of organic disease is incomplete, certain causative factors are well established.

Biological predisposition may be a factor. In some people more than others, colonic activity may be more susceptible to disturbance. There seems to be some tendency for the irritable bowel syndrome to run in families.

In the particularly susceptible, many agents may irritate the colon and trigger symptoms. In some cases, coffee, alcohol, spices, salads, and certain other foods can provoke attacks. There are those who are allergic or highly sensitive to certain foods. Milk-sugar intolerance, for example, is a common problem, but one readily treated by avoidance of milk and milk products.

As many as half of all the people with abdominal complaints have "nervous" gut.

Infections, acute illness, environmental factors, or even a weather change may bring on symptoms.

There is some evidence that inadequate dietary fiber may be a factor for millions of Americans who eat highly refined, overprocessed carbohydrates. In some cases, benefits have been reported from a switch to a high-fiber diet or from the use of a high-fiber supplement such as bran.

But there is no question about the role of stress. "In most patients," reports the American Digestive Disease Society, "the symptoms stem chiefly from emotional stress."

It has been noted that stress is commonly associated with the appearance of symptoms and that still more stress exacerbates the symptoms. Some studies have even shown that symptoms sometimes correlate with a victim's particular mood; that patients experiencing pain and constipation are full of anger while, in contrast, patients with diarrhea are more anxious and feel helpless; and the very same patient may have both types of symptoms, depending upon his or her mood.

## "Is That All It Is?"

Some victims of the irritable bowel may find it difficult to believe that a functional problem, without organic disease, can be responsible for all their symptoms.

Nor does any competent physician hastily jump to such a diagnosis. All other diseases that may cause the same symptoms must be excluded.

In patients with symptoms that are clearly due to emotional stress, all that may be needed is a thorough history and a physical examination. In others, more thorough checks may be needed, including x-rays, instrument examination of the colon, and stool analysis for the presence of blood and infectious or parasitic agents.

## Treating the Irritable Bowel

Treatment, of course, will vary with the individual patient and circumstances. In some, but not all cases, drugs to relieve symptoms that are very acute may be used. Sometimes a mild sedative or an antispasmodic drug is helpful.

If there is any reason to suspect that some particular food may be contributing to the bowel disturbance, its elimination may help. As already noted, increasing fiber intake may be valuable in some cases.

Unless a patient is deeply disturbed, psychotherapy is rarely needed. The patient's realization that stress can easily upset the digestive system can eliminate worry about the possibility of a serious condition, and therefore is often helpful in reducing tension.

Beyond that, any adjustments or modifications that can be made in work, family and social relations, and lifestyle in order to reduce stress can be rewarding. Also, use can be made of other effective techniques for coping with remaining stress. These techniques will be discussed in Chapters 9 and 10.

## Peptic Ulcer

### Is It Really the "Executive Wound Stripe"?

So it's been frequently called. But the definition is a myth.

Executives get ulcers. So do a lot of other people. Although the incidence of ulcer in this country has been declining a little, the disease still affects 10 percent of the population at some time in life. There are estimates that more than 20 million Americans now have, or have had, the problem.

But any idea that ulcer disease is limited to people in high-pressure jobs has been—or certainly should have been—outmoded years ago. One possible reason for the notion that it is the hard-driving executive who gets the ulcer may be the executive's greater likelihood to seek medical care promptly.

Blue-collar workers as well as executives get ulcers. Several investigators have found that deaths from ulcer are more common in people at the lower socioeconomic levels than in those at higher levels. Looking at occupations, one study found that streetcar conductors show the highest incidence of ulcers. Another study, in Norway, found that fishermen have the highest rate in that country.

There are still many puzzles surrounding peptic ulcer. One is why ulcer symptoms peak in autumn and spring; another is why bleeding from an ulcer is most frequent between September and January. Another puzzle is new: why has ulcer incidence dropped over the past few decades?

Ulcers were almost unknown in Europe before 1900. In England there were only about 70 known cases during the entire nineteenth century. But they started increasing about the time of the First World War and by World War II had become an extraordinarily common disease.

Nobody knows why the incidence started to decline. Certainly stress has not decreased. In England during World War II, the number of cases of perforated ulcers, so bad that the acid had eaten completely through the lining of the stomach or duodenum, increased in the cities that the Germans were bombing. When the Nazis shifted their bombing sites, perforated ulcers increased in people who lived in the new target locations.

But none of these observations means that stress plays no role in ulcer development. It can be very much in the picture along with other factors.

## The Hole and the Gnawing

An ulcer is simply an open sore, a hole or erosion, that can occur anywhere in or on the body. But the most common type is the peptic ulcer. There are two types of peptic ulcer: duodenal and gastric.

Duodenal ulcers are found in the duodenum, the first part of the small intestine, lying just outside the stomach. They are about 10 times more common than gastric ulcer—ulcer of the stomach.

Pain is the most common symptom. Usually, it is not sharp but, rather, a gnawing or burning sensation somewhat like a hunger pang. The pain of a gastric ulcer will come on a

# Pain is the most common symptom of an ulcer.

half-hour to 2 hours after a meal; that of a duodenal ulcer, 2 to 4 hours after eating.

The cause of the pain is unclear, but it may be related to the corrosive action of acid and pepsin on the open sore in the empty stomach or duodenum. It is often relieved by eating or by an antacid that neutralizes the acid.

Although ulcers themselves are not killers, about 12,000 Americans die each year from complications. Internal bleeding can occur when an ulcer erodes an artery. Or an ulcer can perforate the stomach or duodenum, allowing contents to leak out and cause peritonitis, a serious inflammation. An ulcer can cause internal swelling, thus obstructing vital passages.

## Ulcer Causes

Many details of the ulcer mechanism have yet to be worked out. But some are clear.

The stomach secretes hydrochloric acid to aid digestion. Even when the stomach is empty, there is a normal intermittent flow of the acid; after a meal, there is a much greater flow. The acid, strong enough to dissolve even iron, does not dissolve the stomach itself because of the protective effect of

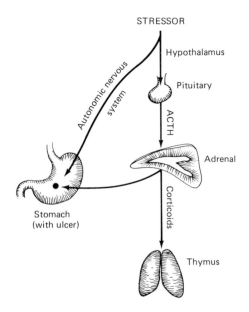

*Principal pathways mediating the response to a stressor. From Hans Selye, Stress Without Distress, J. B. Lippincott, Philadelphia, 1974.*

the mucus secreted by the mucus glands. There is also mucus protection in the duodenum.

An ulcer may develop if there is an excess secretion of acid by the stomach or an alteration of the mucus coating.

Some ulcer patients have been found to have 2 to 4 times as many acid-secreting cells as normal. One possibility is that the large number may result from hereditary influences. Another is that extra cell formation may occur because impulses through the vagus nerves are excessive, calling for increased acid secretions, which may trigger development of more cells in response to demand.

Overactivity of the vagus nerve leading to excessive acid secretion sometimes may result from disease elsewhere—diabetes or chronic lung disease, for example. Acid production may also be increased by alcohol and smoking.

And emotional stress, including aggravation, anxiety, and worry, can trigger the vagus nerve that connects the brain and stomach.

Some studies have indicated increased anxiety in ulcer patients; others have shown that acute stress preceded the onset of ulcer. But many people under even prolonged stress do not develop ulcers.

It appears that stress, or, more accurately, inadequate coping with stress, can play a significant role in ulcer formation, especially when coupled with other factors, including heredity. (Ulcers are about 3 times more common in close relatives of afflicted persons than in the general population.)

## Ulcer Healing

Ulcer treatment is directed at facilitating healing.

Often, the key measure is intensive antacid therapy. Antacids, which neutralize hydrochloric acid, have been found

Acid production may be increased by alcohol and smoking.

# ACHIEVING YOUR FIRST "WOUND STRIPE"

Writing in the *Medical Annals of the District of Columbia* some time ago, Dr. William T. Gibb had some advice on getting an ulcer—the executive's "wound stripe." We summarize it here:

- Forget everything but your job. It comes first and your family understands why you have no time for them and appreciates what you are doing.
- Weekends and holidays are excellent times for work at the office. The family members can go to the beach by themselves.
- Carry your briefcase with you always. Thus, you can review all problems and worries of the day.
- Never turn down any request that might even remotely further your career. Grab all invitations to meetings, dinners, and committees.
- Recreation is a waste of time unless it's with customers or business associates. Time spent at the nineteenth hole is the best of all.
- Don't delegate responsibility. You can do it best. Carry the whole load.
- If you have to travel, work all day and drive or fly all night to the next appointment. Take a few "uppers" so you can be fresh the next morning.
- Be a joiner. Always seek office. It may add a few customers.

- A couple or three quick martinis before dinner is fine for the appetite. No need to relax and chat with the family for half an hour.
- A quick drink before a conference or deal clears your mind and adds to your alertness. Drink along with your luncheon companions; maybe one of them will get a little tight and sign a bigger order.
- Eat only when you are hungry; it's what healthy wild animals do. Lots of gravy and rich desserts are what an active executive needs.
- Never mind doctors; they just want to turn you into a sissy. You're strong as an ox; those height-weight charts do not apply to you.
- Crack the whip constantly on your subordinates. That will keep them alert and make them admire you.
- Take a pep pill or two during the day for extra energy and a good sedative before bed because you're all keyed up by the day's events.

   If you have followed these suggestions, observed Dr. Gibb, you may already have your ulcer—and maybe high blood pressure as well.

to be most effective when taken 1 hour after meals and at bedtime.

Other medication sometimes may be prescribed if needed: anticholinergic drugs that inhibit acid secretion; antispasmodic agents that relax stomach and intestinal muscles; and sedatives. Now in common use is a fairly new drug, cimetidine, a type of antihistamine that is a powerful inhibitor of acid secretion.

The traditional diet of milk, crackers, and other soft, bland foods, long rigidly prescribed for ulcers, has largely been scrapped. Evidence has accumulated that shows such a diet does not work and that, in some patients, it may be so burdensome that it leads to production of even more acids than rich spicy food.

Many physicians now encourage ulcer patients to eat almost anything they enjoy. What possibly should be avoided, however, are alcohol, drinks containing caffeine (coffee, tea, cola) and aspirin, which stimulates acid secretion.

When medical treatment fails or when there is a threatening complication, surgery may be required.

## Is Psychotherapy Necessary?

Unless there is a severe, deep-seated neurosis, psychotherapy is probably not required. But stress factors are important in determining response to the treatment of an ulcer and the likelihood of its recurrence.

The distinguished Walter C. Alvarez, M.D., of the Mayo Clinic, observed:

Stress, or more accurately, inadequate coping with stress, can play a significant role in ulcer formation.

## Many physicians now encourage ulcer patients to eat almost anything they enjoy.

Commonly the biggest factor in the production of an ulcer is a psychic one. A hundred times, after a patient has been operated on, I have seen him get a new and terrible ulcer as soon as he ran into a new emotional jam. And a hundred times, I have seen a man lose his ulcer symptoms the day he achieved mental peace.

It can be vital for an ulcer victim to understand the stressful factors involved in this condition and to adopt effective techniques of remedying or modifying them or of coping with them positively.

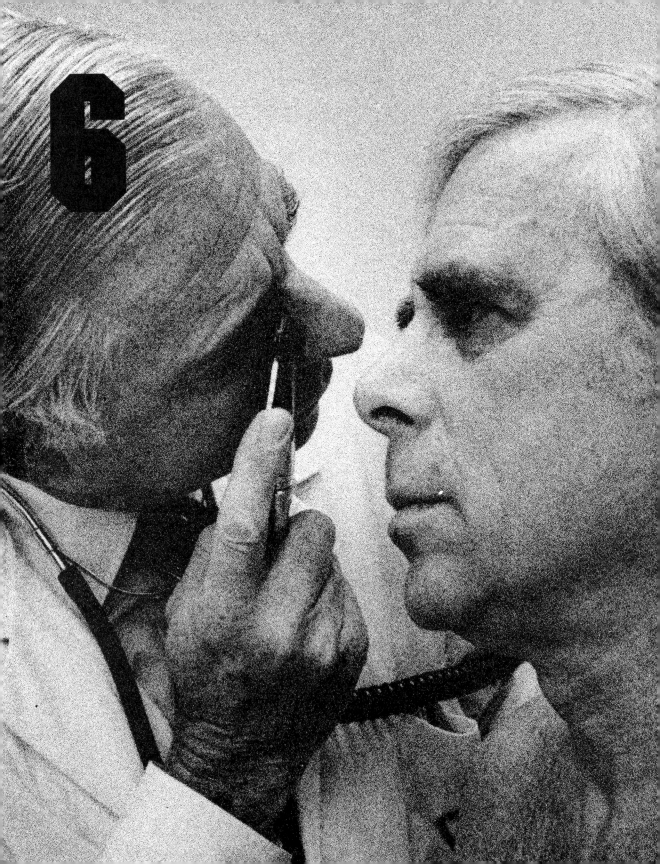

6

# HEADACHES, BACKACHES, NECKACHES: THE STRESS INFLUENCE

An enterprising pharmaceutical firm, one that specializes in developing prescription drugs for headaches, recently conducted a survey to determine whether people in some jobs get headaches more often than those in others.

"One of the things we wanted to know was whether or not life in the boardroom causes headaches," remarked an executive of the drug company. "And we discovered that more often than not, it does."

The survey found that 90 percent of chief executives experience headaches regularly, while the average for the general population is 70 percent. The majority of the executives reported having two to four headaches a week, each one lasting between 1 and 2 hours. But, perhaps to the drug company's dismay, while 80 percent use nonprescription remedies, less than 20 percent use prescription painkillers.

Are the survey results valid? Are there that many headaches at the top?

Others involved in headache research agree. "If you sent questionnaires to everyone who made $200,000 and up, you'd probably find that 90 percent of them were headache sufferers," remarks Dr. Fred Sheftel, a cofounder of the New England Center for Headaches.

"The corporate world is not necessarily one that pins medals on individuals who are footloose and fancy-free," Dr. Sheftel adds. "Control of feelings is prized. Particularly anger. And anger, when suppressed, gives rise to tension headaches."

But these problems are scarcely limited just to top executives; they are frequent and sometimes chronic among executives from the lower levels up. Not just headaches, but neckaches and backaches as well, are among their most common afflictions.

## The Nationwide Headache: Headaches

An estimated 45 million Americans (one-fifth of the population) suffer from severe and sometimes disabling headaches. They lose 124 million workdays a year at a cost of $6.2 billion. They spend $1.2 billion on headache remedies, most often aspirin and related compounds. Headache was the

If you should question everyone who makes $200,000 and up, you'd probably find that 90 percent of them are headache sufferers.

principal cause of an estimated 18,341,923 visits to physicians during 1977–1978, the latest period for which the National Center for Health Statistics has figures.

Headaches, as you might suspect, come in many varieties. Some can be indications of such potentially catastrophic illness as brain tumor, cerebral hemorrhage, or meningitis. But such headaches are relatively uncommon.

There are some queer varieties, or so they may seem. You can get headaches from excessive caffeine intake in the form of coffee, tea, or cola drinks. We have known chronic sufferers who have been amazed at their freedom from "browbusters" once they have cut back from 6, 8, or 10 cups of coffee and several cola drinks daily.

But it is not only too *much* caffeine that can produce headaches; too *little* can sometimes be responsible. So, if you are a heavy imbiber and want to cut down, do so gradually.

For example, there is now an explanation for why some people have weekend and holiday headaches. Late sleeping leads to early morning deprivation—and headaches—in those used to large amounts of caffeine-containing beverages taken early in the morning on weekdays.

Caffeine withdrawal can also account for the headaches of many people who, for religious or other reasons, fast even for just one day. One way of getting relief is to use a suppository containing 150 milligrams of caffeine, prepared by a pharmacist on prescription, on the morning of the fast.

The explanation may seem bizarre, but sleeping with bedcovers pulled up over the head is a recently reported headache cause. Called the "turtle headache" by the physician who literally uncovered it, it produces pain all over the head, but is greatest in front. Some of the victims are awakened by it during the night; others get it on awakening. Cure for the problem, which may be the result of oxygen shortage, is to keep the covers below one's head.

There are also the headaches caused by eating cured meats. Such meats (frankfurters, bacon, salami, ham) often contain nitrites, chemical preservatives. In the nitrite-sensitive person, they can kick off trouble.

But by far the most common form of headaches are migraine (affecting some 15 million Americans) and tension headaches affecting close to 30 million). In both these types stress is a major factor.

### *Tension (Muscle Contraction) Headache*

It's a generalized, steady ache. The pain is dull, bandlike. Some victims describe the pain as a feeling of tightness or as a sensation that the neck and upper back are in a cast. The headache may last for several hours, occur daily, several times a week, or several times a month. Records at some headache clinics indicate that 30 percent of patients have at least one headache a day and 20 percent have constant pain.

The tension headache, the most common kind, is related to chronic contraction of muscles about the head and neck. The reason that such muscle contraction produces headache is simple to understand. If you were to clench your fist tightly and keep it clenched, you would feel an ache very soon. And with prolonged clenching, you would develop pain similar to that of headache.

When a job requires a fixed head position—for example, because of driving against bright headlights—we often set the muscles of neck, jaw, and scalp in pain-causing postures.

But we commonly do the same thing as part of a reaction to stress. One theory holds that the setting, the muscle contraction, may be a trait carried over from our early ancestors and associated with their fight-or-flight reaction. Great apes, for example, upon assuming an aggressive stance, commonly tighten muscles to pull their heads down between their shoulders.

Tension headache victims have been said to "symbolically carry a great weight on their shoulders." Upon feeling anxiety, boredom, frustration, harassment, or other reactions to stress, they may set neck, jaw, and scalp muscles and thus develop a headache.

Muscle contraction almost always accompanies migraine. One fact, often unappreciated, is that a migraine sufferer may get muscle contraction headaches as well—combined with, as well as separate from, migraine headaches.

# Muscle contraction almost always accompanies migraine.

## Migraine

While tension headaches often appear late in the day as pressures mount, migraine may start on awakening in the morning.

Actually, there are two forms of migraine: classical and common.

The *classical* starts with constriction of blood vessels. At that point there is no pain. In this prodromal period, fore-runner to the headache, there are sensory disturbances such as the perception of supposedly flashing lights or other visual abnormalities including blind spots. Some victims complain of frequency of urination at this point.

Then, in about half an hour, the blood vessel constriction is succeeded by blood vessel dilation. Now comes the pain. It's mostly one-sided, often toward the eye, aching or throb-bing, beating with the pulse. Often it's accompanied by nau-sea, vomiting, and sensitivity to light, so the victim seeks a darkened room if possible.

*Common* migraine develops without the prodrome of vi-sual phenomena. The pain of common migraine is as likely to be on both sides of the head as on one.

Migraine can be induced by factors other than stress. Certain foods, including chocolate, nuts, citrus juice in large quantities, and aged cheese, as well as alcoholic drinks, can trigger an attack. Rapid changes in hormone levels, as some women experience during ovulation or before menstruation, can account for migraine. So can rapid change in blood sugar level, as in people after oversleeping or fasting.

But stress is the major initiating factor in migraine, al-though the migraine attack often does not begin until the stress is over. And this occurrence of headache following, rather than during, stress, some authorities maintain, can be a distinguishing feature of migraine.

## Combating Chronic Headaches

For a tension headache, heat, massage, a hot shower, an aspirin or another pain reliever often helps.

Once a migraine attack occurs, ergotamine tartrate may be used to cut it short. In some cases, another drug as well —aspirin or another analgesic—may be needed to affect the accompanying tension headache.

Drug therapy may be helpful in staving off future attacks of migraine. Recently, the drug propranolol (Inderal), an agent often used for high blood pressure, has come into increasing use as a preventive to migraine.

## THE TWO MOST COMMON HEADACHES

|  | Tension, or muscle contraction | Migraine |
|---|---|---|
| Onset | Commonly at ages 30 to 60 but often begins with occasional episodes in early adulthood | Childhood to early adulthood; uncommon after 40 |
| Sex | Male and female | 3 females to 1 male |
| Location | Generalized, like a tight band around head | Often forehead; usually on one side; sometimes alternating sides, or both sides at once |
| Frequency | Several times a week or daily, often on weekends, holidays | Commonly 2 to 4 a month, but may occur only a few times a year |
| Duration | Continuous through day | 2 hours to 3 or 4 days |
| Intensity | Mild to severe; usually dull, nonthrobbing | Moderate to severe; usually throbbing; often incapacitating |
| Other symptoms | Neck tightness; feelings of anxiety or depression | Nausea, vomiting, sometimes visual disturbances |
| Trigger factors | Stress, emotional upsets | Stress; fatigue; lack of sleep; hunger; weather changes; some foods |

# Migraine can be induced by factors other than stress.

In victims of chronic tension headaches, mental depression is sometimes a factor. Treatment with an antidepressant drug may relieve both the headaches and the depression.

When at all possible, even if not easy, the victim's best means of combating stress-related headaches of either type is to determine the causative stressors and eliminate or avoid them if feasible or to learn to cope with them more effectively.

Biofeedback, as we shall see in Chapter 10, can be of great value for many chronic headache victims, providing control often without need for drugs.

## The Aching Back

If the estimates are right, on any day in the United States, some 6.5 million people are victims of backache.

The bad back has even become somewhat fashionable, a kind of "in" misery. "It has emerged," observed a popular magazine article some years ago, "as such a status symbol that sufferers boldly and openly proclaim their affliction by the way they stand—with pelvis thrust forward and one hand held casually astern in the vicinity of the fifth lumbar region."

It has been said, too, that backache has become "in" almost because of a prevailing idea that once a sufferer, always a sufferer, and that, if you have to live with an affliction, you might as well be proud of it.

A cliché would have it that ever since humans stood upright on two legs instead of crawling around on all fours, they were doomed to ache behind. But, since millions maneuver through life without ever having a twinge, the inevitability thesis has to be considered with some skepticism.

There is also an idea that once a backache victim, ipso facto, always a victim. A common notion seems to be that there are no practical known ways to avoid backaches. Most stem from "slipped" or ruptured disks, which means surgery, which is hopeless.

But all these assertions are nonsense.

### The 81 Percent Likelihood

To be sure, a backache can come from a herniated disk.

The spinal column, or backbone, is a column of separate bones or vertebrae—33 of them stacked upward from the sacrum to the base of the skull. Within them is the spinal cord with its nerve cables emerging from the brain. Between each vertebra and the next is a disk, a circular cushion of connective tissue and cartilage, roughly $\frac{1}{4}$- to $\frac{3}{4}$- inch thick. The disks serve to absorb the impact of body weight and movements.

In themselves, vertebrae have no stability. Ligaments, tough and fibrous, run between them and bind them together. But more than ligaments are needed to keep the spinal column upright. Muscle action is required. It is so necessary that fainting, which interrupts muscle activity, results in immediate collapse.

There are some 140 muscles attached to the spine and they perform prodigious work. Say you weigh 180 pounds and bend forward. The muscle force needed to keep you from toppling over will be 450 pounds. And if you are carrying a 50-pound weight, the force will have to be 750 pounds.

The "slipped disk" you hear so much about is really a misnomer. A disk does not slip. Actually, in the case of a so-

On any day in the United States, some 6.5 million people are victims of backache.

# The most common cause of recurrent backaches is muscle tension.

called slip, the rim of the disk weakens and tears, and part of the soft, gelatinlike center, the nucleus pulposus, becomes extruded. The extruded (herniated) portion may press on sensitive nerve roots, producing pain.

A disk can herniate when its tough outer rim is injured severely enough—suddenly, during a bad fall or other seri-

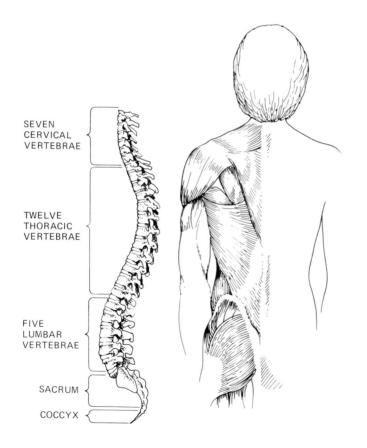

SEVEN
CERVICAL
VERTEBRAE

TWELVE
THORACIC
VERTEBRAE

FIVE
LUMBAR
VERTEBRAE

SACRUM

COCCYX

*The powerful muscles that are attached to the spine contract as the body moves, sometimes loading the spine heavily. Usually backaches come from strain on these muscles and can disappear quickly. But repeated stressing can affect the spine itself.*

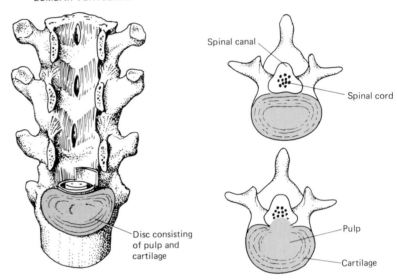

LUMBAR VERTEBRAE

Spinal canal

Spinal cord

Disc consisting
of pulp and
cartilage

Pulp

Cartilage

*The discs act as cushions between the movable vertebrae of the back. A disc that "slips" may press on a nerve and cause pain and disability.*

ous accident, or gradually, through years of constant jarring activity.

Pain may originate, too, from arthritic changes in the spine. Occasionally, it may arise from conditions removed from the spine—for example, gallbladder disease, peptic ulcer, colitis, sometimes even heart disease.

But in the great majority of cases, backache has nothing to do with any of these conditions.

Some years ago, 5000 consecutive cases of back pain were studied by a combined medical group from New York and Columbia Universities. In 81 percent of the cases—somewhat more than 4000 of the 5000—the backaches were related to muscle problems.

# The bad back has become somewhat fashionable.

## The Clenched Muscle Factor

The most common cause of recurrent backaches is muscle tension, or spasm.

Muscle spasm means continued, involuntary contractions of muscle. If you have ever experienced an eye tic, for example, you have had one, usually minor, form of spasm.

Spasm can have useful purposes. If a joint, for example, is injured, muscles about the joint will contract and stay contracted, serving as a kind of splint to protect the joint. If a muscle is injured or under excessive strain, it may go into spasm, and so may other nearby muscles, in an effort to splint the strained muscle and thus to prevent further damage.

Spasm can be very painful. The pain results from lack of nutrition. In muscle, as in other body tissues, blood carrying oxygen and nutrients come in through arteries; after delivering its cargo, it picks up waste products from muscle cells and leaves through veins. It is through thin-walled capillaries, very tiny vessels lying between arteries and veins, that oxygen and nutrients move from blood to muscle cells and in turn move waste from cells to blood.

When muscles contract, capillaries are squeezed shut. Normally, the contraction is brief and the exchange of material goes on normally. But with spasm, the exchange process is impaired. Waste products, including lactic acid, can produce pain when they remain in a muscle. Lactic acid, especially, is an irritant to nerve endings. Moreover, a muscle in spasm is working, since it is contracting, and the lack of oxygen causes muscle tissues to cry out in pain.

## Spasm and Stress

Muscle spasm can be induced by injury or excessive demand. Strain a back muscle by lifting a heavy load—or even a moderate one in the wrong fashion—and you can expect spasm.

Excessive demand on muscles is not a matter only of lifting. You have seen guy wires supporting a telephone pole. Stomach muscles act somewhat like guy wires for the spinal

# In 81 percent of cases, backaches were related to muscle problems.

column. When these muscles are weak, as they commonly are because of lack of adequate exercise, we have a tendency to fall backward. But we maintain balance by shifting body weight, leaning forward slightly, and hanging our weight on muscles of the back. This solution, however, puts excessive loading or demand on these muscles. They can become fatigued, a condition that increases the likelihood of spasm.

Moreover, emotional tension can induce spasm, and it commonly does. It arouses muscle tension, which is a normal biological response to emotional tension. Muscles tense to make possible fighting or fleeing. But in many instances, however provoked we are by emotional stress, we can neither fight nor flee. Our bodies are prepared for physical action of some kind but we take none—at least, none of the fighting or fleeing kind.

Nevertheless, our muscles tense in the situation, and they may remain tense, in a state of semicontraction, even during sleep, for days, weeks, or months.

This is chronic muscle spasm. Depending upon the muscles most sensitive and most involved, it may lead to headache or neckache or backache. It is a very common factor in backache.

Stress, sometimes enough in itself to trigger spasm and pain, often is a compounding influence. Over a period of time, a chronically tensed muscle can shorten and lose its stretch; this limitation may induce painful conditions. It can also lead to awkward movements, which would make the muscles more susceptible to injury.

## Combating Backache

Stress-related backache can be prevented, and it can be combated once it occurs.

The immediate cause of pain, as we have noted, is spasm. Not only does the spasm lead to pain; a vicious cycle can be set up, with the pain then leading to more spasm, which, in turn, can lead to still more pain.

For relief, both spasm and pain must be attacked.

A backache attack, even a severe one, often can be relieved with relatively simple home remedies if they are used properly. But aspirin or an equivalent pain reliever is not likely to be enough. Taking a pain reliever should be the first step, but treatment should not stop there.

\* *Lie down with as little delay as possible. Apply heat, using a heating pad wrapped in a Turkish towel. After 30 minutes or so, change position to avoid stiffness. (For some people, cold may provide quicker relief than heat; if you are one of these people, gently rub the painful area with ice cubes or crushed ice in a pillowcase.)*

\* *Follow this treatment with a gentle rubdown of the painful area with any commercially available counterirritant.*

\* *Continue taking aspirin or its equivalent, such as acetaminophen, two tablets every 3 to 4 hours as needed.*

\* *Repeat the hot or cold applications. If heat helps and you can get into a tub, take a 30-minute hot bath and repeat several times.*

\* *By the next day, you may find the pain beginning to ease. Continue the pain reliever and the hot or cold applications. As the pain lessens, begin gentle exercises, moving arms and legs, arching and curving the back.*

It is the combination of measures, directed at the spasm as well as the pain, that often works.

## Why Not Try Prevention?

Exercise looms large in prevention.

First of all, it can strengthen abdominal muscles and thus help to ease any excessive demand on back muscles. The exercise may well include graduated sit-ups.

Exercise also can help as a means of relieving muscle tension when it develops in response to stress. Such exercise can consist of brisk walking, jogging, rope skipping, tennis, badminton, or another sport. Next time you get "hot under the collar" and feel tension mounting, try getting up from your desk and simply walking about for 5 minutes even within your office. Better yet, get outside and take a fast 10-minute walk.

H.B. is a 33-year-old junior executive for a prestigious bank. He commutes to and from work an hour each way on the train. He has noticed that since he got married and moved to the suburbs, he has been slowly gaining weight and is now 10 to 15 pounds over his college weight. With his job pressures increasing, he has not taken ample time to stay fit with regular exercise.

Six months ago, H.B. was promoted. Since that time, he has been working under a different manager, who, he told his EHE doctor during his annual checkup, has been making his life pretty rough with increasing numbers of presentations, deadlines, etc. He has been more irritable, arguing with colleagues and snapping at his wife. This lack of control has led to a deteriorating self-image; he has increasingly doubted his ability to withstand the pressures and to succeed in his chosen career. Physical symptoms of rapid heartbeat, sweaty palms, and muscle tightness have been frequent.

The results of his entire physical exam and laboratory work were normal, indicating that H.B. was basically healthy except for his moderate overweight condition and a borderline high blood pressure (145/90). The EHE doctor felt strongly that H.B. could significantly improve his image and self-confidence as well as blunt his exaggerated response to stress if he could undertake a program of regular, vigorous

# The pain of a spasm results from lack of nutrition for the muscle.

exercise. Since lack of time was a key factor because of the commuting, the EHE doctor assisted H.B. in finding an exercise facility complete with bicycles, treadmills, and a variety of other equipment only a few blocks from his office.

After 4 months, H.B. is happily exercising for an hour during lunch time 3 days a week. His manager has commented on his demeanor and noticeably improving physique. H.B. now thrives on the stresses to which he used to submit. His physician is gratified with his lowered blood pressure (130/82) and his low pulse rate.

Biofeedback, which we mentioned earlier, may also be of value as a means of augmenting relaxation.

But there are still other helpful methods of coping positively with stress, which we shall discuss in Chapters 9 and 10.

## Neck Pain

Another favorite target of stress-induced chronic muscle tension, as we have noted, are the muscles of the head and neck, with resultant tension headaches.

Some people develop toothaches from the tension of jaw muscles. If this tension goes on long enough, bones in the gums may be affected and premature tooth loss may result.

Neck pain, too—with or without headache—commonly involves stress-induced muscle tension. Chronic neck pain almost invariably stems directly from persistent spasm of neck muscles. This is the spasm that can develop as the result of acute muscle stretch from whiplash movement of the head in an accident. It sometimes arises from irritation of the nerve roots supplying the neck muscles, with the irritation coming from osteoarthritis of the spine in the neck region.

It may also be the result of, or may be aggravated by, stress.

Stress-induced spasm often affects the trapezius muscle, which runs from the middle of the back up the tips of the shoulders and attaches to the occipital protuberances, two projections of bone on the lower part of the back of the skull.

When the trapezius goes into spasm, it can tug strongly on the periosteal covering of the skull, a fibrous membrane, producing painful constricting headaches. When in spasm, it can also produce neck pain and, sometimes, pain in the upper back.

And there are many opportunities for the trapezius to go into spasm.

You may have noted that a cat, when alarmed or otherwise disturbed by something, usually arches its back and hunches its shoulders. In this way, it is preparing to pounce or to flee. We humans go through much the same procedure even if not so obviously. Often, we tend to elevate the shoulders just a bit when under stress. Even though not very great, the elevation can be enough to contract the trapezius muscle. And, like any other muscle, the trapezius, if contracted long enough, can go into spasm.

### Combating Neck Pain

If you suffer from frequent neck pain caused by tension, you might try relatively simple measures to help reduce their frequency and severity.

* *On any day, and especially on a day full of stress, take a brief time out to elevate your shoulders. Bring them up close to your ears, then shake them down. Wiggle your shoulders up and around. Roll your head around, too, in gentle circles. In carrying out these movements, you are, of course, contracting muscles. But you are also causing the muscles to relax and the relaxation helps to prevent spasm.*

* *If spasm-induced neck pain does appear, keep in mind that as the spasm triggers pain, the pain in turn leads to more spasms. The cycle must be interrupted as soon as possible. In addition to aspirin or another pain reliever, the technique mentioned earlier for relieving muscle spasm affecting the back often can be used effectively for relieving tension neck pain.*

✴ *Heat or cold can be applied to the trapezius muscle in the back of the neck. A counterirritant, too, may be used, often more effectively when it follows heat application.*

✴ *Massage can be useful. With your fingertips, rub the area from the back of your skull down your neck and across the top of your shoulders, repeating the procedure several times.*

7

# THE MENTAL AND EMOTIONAL TOLLS

When A.L., a 41-year-old sales executive consulted his physician at Executive Health Examiners, he complained of headaches that had begun about a month earlier and had recurred almost daily. But it soon developed that there was more to his story.

A.L. looked anxious. He was restless and tense. As he was gently prodded to reveal any other complaints he might have, he began to talk about them—hesitatingly and in a voice that occasionally quavered. He spoke of sometimes feeling suddenly apprehensive with no reason, of fatigue and sleeping difficulty, of episodes of chest tightness and pain.

When he finally let go, he talked of having problems with his work, of feeling sluggish about it, of growing indecisiveness.

A.L. was a victim of anxiety. And he was typical of many such victims in our society where what we see as physical illness is considered more respectable than so-called mental illness. Like many people to whom symptoms of apparent physical origin are more acceptable than those considered emotional, he had, for some time, endured the consequences of stress while they were mainly emotional. He sought help only when he could consider himself "sick"— with headaches.

Stress can provoke emotional or psychological reactions as often as it can provoke physical ones. It can trigger anxiety. It can trigger depression. And, not uncommonly, it can lead to a mix of both. A.L. was referred for psychological counseling to help him understand his underlying problems and to learn better coping methods.


# Anxiety


## *The Normal and Abnormal*

Anxiety can sometimes be defined as a diffuse, unpleasant, often vague feeling of apprehension.

It can be that and no more, or that and much more.

All of us, quite normally, experience anxiety. We have our moments of frustration, inner turmoil, or disquietude in reaction to quite ordinary stressors of life ranging from an argument with the boss or a run-in at home perhaps to the loss of a friend.

Anxiety over a coming event, with concern about the outcome or about handling oneself well, is certainly not unusual. An interview, an examination, a party—there's an almost infinite line of anxiety-triggering situations in ordinary life. "Butterflies" before giving a speech, tension and a queasy stomach before seeing a vitally important client— such discomfort is common. In fact, feelings such as these can actually perform a service as indicators of hormonal activity arousing the body and energizing it for accomplishment.

Fortunately, they are temporary feelings from which we usually recover quickly. We bounce back from such anxiousness.

On the other hand, anxiety can be of another kind—an aura, a cloud of anxiety, nonspecific, pervasive. It has been referred to as "free-floating." It hovers, for no apparent reason, allowing even a minor crisis to kindle strong feelings of dread.


## *In the Grip*

Anxiety is capable of producing a wide range of physical and psychological symptoms. No victim is likely to suffer all;

"Most of the stressful situations confronted by our patients can be remedied and the problems resolved by making use of the self-help aids for relaxation and lifestyle changes that we recommend.

"Some patients, however, present warning signs that we consider serious enough to suggest a referral to the director of our stress control center. We have found that when a patient follows up on our recommendation for a deeper look into the problem, it can almost always be resolved successfully."

an Executive Health Examiners physician

# BEYOND STRESS— WHEN THE RED FLAG GOES UP

Do you feel, or have you experienced lately, any of the following:

- feeling of worthlessness at work and at home
- the thought that you can't seem to do anything right lately
- doubt in the value of your career and life in general
- extreme irritability; easy explosiveness
- reluctance to face each new day
- fatigue and depression when you wake up, even after ample sleep

- the increasing need for alcohol or pills such as sleeping pills and tranquilizers
- feeling of desperation and wanting to get away from it all
- separation or divorce
- problems with children, such as teenager on drugs
- geographic relocation, especially abroad
- sickness or death in the family
- changing jobs, release, or demotion

some experience only a few. But some people are disturbed by many unexplained feelings.

A person may have a feeling of being wound up, on edge, fearful without reason. Common tasks, even that of going to a dinner party or visiting a friend, may be dreaded. Decision making can be difficult. There may be a barrier to concentration and a failure of recall. One may be restless by day and experience sleep-disturbing restlessness at night. Nightmares may occur. Often, one's tolerance for frustration may

# Anxiety is capable of producing a wide range of physical and psychological symptoms.

be lowered and there may be angry outbursts about relatively minor setbacks.

Physical symptoms may include easy fatigability, shortness of breath, chest pain, palpitations. One's appetite may be disturbed and one may have uncomfortable feelings of fullness after meals, sometimes with vomiting episodes. When an important decision is to be made or some critical situation has to be faced, anticipatory diarrhea may occur.

The victim of anxiety may experience attacks of hyperventilation, or overbreathing. In hyperventilation, breathing may be abnormally prolonged and deep. The overbreathing is not necessarily apparent to the victim or to onlookers. Because of the excessive breathing, there is an abnormally large loss of carbon dioxide in the expired air, which results in a biochemical disturbance called respiratory alkalosis.

The alkalosis can cause such symptoms as lightheadedness, scalp and neck tightness, tingling and burning sensations, chest pain, palpitations, faintness, spells of dizziness, smothering sensations, throat fullness, and pain over the stomach region.

Often, the victim can quickly relieve an attack of hyperventilation by holding a paper bag over his or her nose and breathing in and out until the carbon dioxide level is returned to normal.

## State and Trait

As you may have noticed, and as recent studies have shown, some people seem just naturally more anxious than others.

There are, in fact, according to many investigators, two kinds of anxiety: state and trait.

*State anxiety* is an individual's current, momentary anxiety level. In some cases, it is quite appropriate; the level is at a degree that stimulates mental alertness and helps in making decisions and taking action. In other cases, however, the level is such as to lead to paralyzing apprehension and inability to think clearly or to make even relatively routine daily decisions.

The other type, *trait anxiety,* is a basic or characteristic anxiety. "It may be thought of as an individual's innate susceptibility to anxiety under stressful circumstances, and its level may be a variable that differs within a wide range from one person to another," says Dr. Leo E. Hollister, a professor at Stanford University School of Medicine. "This may well be what, over the long span of human experience, came to be thought of as differences in temperament."

It seems to Hollister that there is a link between anxiety and genetic predisposition that will probably be substantiated by further study. He also points to work already done by Karl Rickels, M.D., of the University of Pennsylvania, in observing and charting the different anxiety levels of normal, apparently nonanxious, individuals and others who have been treated for anxiety and are now free of symptoms.

Rickels found that while treatment with tranquilizers could reduce the symptoms of anxious persons down to a nonsymptom level, it was never the same low or basal level of normal, nonanxious individuals.

Such observations as those of Rickels, suggests Dr. Hollister:*

are why we can appropriately refer to a threshold for anxiety response. People whom we call normal in relation to this symptomatic threshold are people whose reaction to stress tends to remain below the threshold.

On the other hand, a person with a history of anxiety seems to start out closer to the anxiety threshold. That person appears to have less room to maneuver, or less resilience for coping with extraordinary pressures. And in a chronically anxious person, the basic or trait level seems so close to the threshold that even the ordinary pressures of life can sometimes push him beyond his ability to cope.

* Leo E. Hollister, M.D., from seminar on the consequences of stress, New York City, January 1979.

# The victim of anxiety may experience attacks of hyperventilation.

## Help for an Anxious Executive

T.D. was, in a way, a lucky man. At 50, after spending much of his business career with a middlewestern manufacturing firm and achieving the rank of vice president, he suddenly lost his job as the result of a merger.

He considered himself lucky when, after almost a year of searching for a new position, he found one in a Connecticut company which had recently adopted a policy of opening up more positions with advancement opportunities for older executives.

Six months after he was hired, things began to go wrong. He was missing deadlines with some consistency. He appeared to be nervous, tense, indecisive. He took to pacing his office a good part of the day. He smoked heavily, and he complained of severe headaches.

His immediate superior expressed concern. When he was examined by the company's medical department, alcoholism—about which there had been some suspicion—was ruled out as an explanation for what was going on. And when no organic reason for T.D.'s problems could be found, a company physician urged a psychiatric consultation.

In a session with a psychiatrist, T.D. revealed that once before, while in college, he had suffered what he called "a bit of a breakdown." Translated, he had, in fact, gone through an acute anxiety attack. It appeared to have been occasioned when, under the stress of final examinations, he suffered a shock: the accidental death of a close friend. He had come through that, but not without considerable anguish.

Currently, T.D. was suffering from anxiety. There had been the stress of sudden job loss followed by months of unsuccessful job seeking. There had been the stress of relocation when he finally had been successful in finding his new job. Now his wife was having difficulty in finding a new position and one of his two children was having problems in the new school. On top of this, T.D. was finding his new job stressful, considering himself on trial. He was edgy about that and so tense that he had trouble making decisions and meeting deadlines.

For T.D., the psychiatrist decided, what was needed was a combination of a tranquilizing agent and psychotherapy. The drug was recommended for a very limited time to provide some relief of his symptoms; the therapy would be aimed at letting T.D. express his inner feelings and doubts and at providing him with encouragement and reassurance.

In less than a month, he was responding well, and after another several months, was entirely recovered, doing an excellent job and happily reassured by that fact.

## Is Drug Treatment Essential?

Tranquilizers may or may not be necessary in treating anxiety. They may be valuable in acute situations when judiciously used. They do not cure anxiety, but when there is considerable pain or anguish, they may provide enough relief to enable the sufferer to solve problems more easily and to eliminate or moderate the stress and reactions to stress that have triggered anxiety.

# ANXIETY AND A REMARKABLE DISCOVERY

Dr. Hollister has indulged in some intriguing speculation.

Late in the 1970s, he noted, came a remarkable discovery: that the brain actually contains specific receptors for tranquilizing compounds such as diazepam (Valium). These drugs bind to and act on these receptors in proportion to their potency as agents for treating patients with anxiety.

Obviously, the receptors were not put there to wait for Valium or similar compounds to come along. A search was begun to find a material naturally present in the brain that binds to those receptors.

Here there is an obvious analogy to the discovery of endorphins, the natural, opiatelike, pain-relieving materials naturally present in the brain. A natural tranquilizerlike material in the brain might exist in order to regulate the normal level of anxiety much as endorphins modulate pain.

Hollister has remarked: "One could postulate that people with low-level anxiety may have adequate concentrations of this natural substance that may lower their anxiety response level. If this should prove to be the case, it would suggest that people with high-level trait anxiety have been somehow cheated of an adequate supply of this natural substance. This is pure blue-sky speculation, of course. But the story of the natural opiates—the endorphins, which were discovered in the human body as recently as 1975—certainly opens the door to this sort of possibility. Knowledge of brain chemistry is expanding so quickly these days that one can hardly keep up with it."

Whether or not drug treatment is indicated, at Executive Health Examiners we have found that anxiety victims often can be helped significantly by adopting a few basic measures, such as

* *coming to a full realization that stress is a real disorder, capable of creating havoc*

* *getting an understanding of how stress can bring about emotional and physical symptoms*

* *getting reassurance, based on medical examination, that a feared possible organic disease is not actually present*

* *establishing a program of exercise both to improve physical fitness and to help relieve tension, anxiety, and stress*

* *modifying as much as possible, stressful work or other pressures*

Caffeine in excess may play a significant role in some cases of anxiety and of depression.

The physician also determines whether excessive intake of caffeine in various forms (not always obvious) may be a problem. Caffeine in excess has recently been found to play a significant role in some cases of anxiety, and of depression as well.

At a medical seminar devoted to the consequences of stress, a striking case study involving a whole family was presented by Robert E. Rakel, M.D., head of the University of Iowa College of Medicine, Department of Family Practice. Dr. Rakel's report is very much worth presenting here in the following summary:*

Stress can affect an entire family. And early recognition and control can prevent devastating consequences for both individuals and families.

One of the earliest signs of stress in a family is a cluster of symptoms. Family members start coming to a doctor for a variety of physical or emotional complaints.

When I treat members of the same family, I keep a family chart as well as an individual patient chart. One component of the family chart is a family-member visit register. It provides instant chronological documentation of the reasons why different members of the family have come to see me.

Now . . . to the Smith family. This is a large and complicated family. It is a second marriage for both Allan and Rita Smith. They have five children by their former marriages and a sixth by this marriage.

When I met the family 5 years ago, Allan was 31, and the two children from his first marriage were an 11-year-old boy Ronnie, and a 9-year-old girl Kim. Rita was 27, and had three children from her first marriage: Michelle, 10, Daniel, 8, and Amy, 5. Allan and Rita had been married 3 years, and their baby, Jennifer, was a year old.

Soon after they moved to my town, Daniel was brought to my office because of a severe asthma attack, and 2 days later, Michelle was brought in for a similar reason. Three days later, Rita herself came to see me about tension headaches and fatigue. I also learned through these visits that Rita, Michelle, and Daniel had various allergies.

# STRESS AND ANXIETY: A CASE STUDY

---

* Robert E. Rakel, M.D., Seminar on the consequences of stress, New York City, January 1979.

Over the first 6 months, I saw everybody in the family. Daniel and Michelle had recurrent asthma attacks. Rita had a variety of complaints involving various body systems. The other children were showing up in my office with colds and stomach aches. *The frequency and variety of their complaints clearly presented a cluster pattern* of symptoms and strongly indicated the possibility of underlying stress.

This possibility gained support when I learned that the children with asthma had attacks when the parents argued about money. It was confirmed when Rita started talking about her marital problems on her third visit.

She had married Allan because she felt he needed her. She saw herself as a kind of rescuer. But after 3 years of marriage, she decided her own needs weren't being satisfied. Yet she didn't want a divorce. She identified with Allan's children from his first marriage and got along well with them. Both Allan and Rita loved the baby, Jennifer, very much, and divorce would have meant a bitter custody fight.

Once Rita started talking about her personal problems, other family problems emerged—problems of money, school, isolation within the community, and sexual relations.

Rita subsequently insisted that Allan see a doctor. He called my office for a physical examination. It is very common for the husband to be the last member of the family we see. In this case, the last patient to come turned out to need help much more than anyone else.

On the surface, Allan Smith was a quiet, gentle man. At first, my questions about his health and life elicited noncommittal answers.

His nonverbal responses were more revealing. For example, when I asked, "How are things at work?" he first cleared his throat, then rubbed his nose, and finally answered, "Fine."

The throat-clearing and nose rub are avoidance responses. He was saying nonverbally, "I don't like what you're asking me," or "I'm uncomfortable with my answer because things aren't going well." So these signs told me I was touching a sensitive spot.

I paused for a few seconds and then asked, "Are you sure things are fine?"

The mask fell away and Allan opened up with a flood of information about his physical suffering, his problems with his job, and his panic about the possible dissolution of his marriage. Now he started giving fuller answers to questions about his health and life. Some of the symptoms he reported seemed quite definite and specific, others seemed vague and nonspecific. But most important, the symptoms were diffuse and involved different body systems, and they did not suggest any pattern of organic disease.

The first thing he said was that he had felt nervous and tense most of his life. He now felt tired all the time and had trouble falling asleep at night. Sometimes he had attacks of shaking, and during these attacks, his heart raced and he felt dizzy. Lately, he had noticed a sudden waving sensation when he looked at an object. He also had trouble concentrating and felt confused.

His personal medical history showed little physical illness. In his family history there had been hypertension and heart attack problems, and he was worried about these possibilities. On physical examination, however, his blood pressure was normal, 126/84, and so was his electrocardiogram. So I was able to reassure him that heart disease was not the cause of his problem.

The physical examination revealed bilateral hyperactive reflexes and a fast pulse at rest. He had signs of an incipient inguinal hernia, but there were no serious physical findings to explain his troubling symptoms.

As you know, if you look hard enough you can find some sort of physical problem in almost everyone. Such organic red herrings can throw one off the diagnostic trail. That's why it is essential to make a positive diagnosis of anxiety or depression when stress causes an emotional disturbance.

The diagnosis for Allan Smith was acute anxiety, superimposed on a history of chronic anxiety. The factors that pointed to this diagnosis were:

* *a long history of anxiety. He had felt tense or nervous most of his life.*

* *diffuse symptoms that affected different organ systems.*

* *most important, the absence in his symptoms of any recognizable pattern of organic disease.*

* *constant fatigue and trouble falling asleep.*

* *the confirming signs of sympathetic arousal, that is, a fast pulse and hyperactive reflexes.*

During the physical examination, Allan and I had talked about his work. He had been promoted to a supervisory job with an increase in salary, but the new position required a change of location. When he and his wife moved to the new town, they bought a large house and then found that the salary increase did not go as far as they had anticipated. So Rita went to work to help out financially. She was unhappy about working. She preferred to be home taking care of the baby. And baby-sitting costs were eating up a large part of her take-home pay.

Allan felt guilty and overwhelmed in his job. He drank coffee heavily throughout the day and was smoking three packs of cigarettes a day.

The gap between this man's expectations and the reality of his life was a fast-widening chasm. A number of factors played a part. They included a rapid sequence of life-changing events—many milestone changes within a short period of time. He had experienced, first, divorce and sole responsibility for his two children; next, new marriage; then, new job; then, new baby; then, a move to a new city; then, the purchase of a too expensive house.

Allan's job is a good example. He had been promoted above his capacity. He was dealing unsuccessfully with his problems by working longer and longer hours and was becoming increasingly less productive. By the time he got home each night, he was exhausted and irritable.

Allan and Rita argued incessantly about money. That is probably the most common issue in marital strife, because financial stress brings out attitudes toward money that can accentuate the gap between expectation and reality.

The results of this widening gap were reflected in the children's illnesses. Whenever the parents fought over money and related problems, the children got upset. Stress then provoked asthma attacks in Daniel and Michelle. Their condition frightened the parents, and they would unite to care for the children. Soon the children were using their asthma to keep the family together. The manipulation was not conscious, but both children had become aware that when they started wheezing, Mother and Dad stopped fighting. On the other hand, the asthma attacks were serious, and they meant that neither child was under satisfactory medical control.

The family was heading steadily downward in its crisis. So the first objective of management was to gain some control, to buy time for the individuals and the family to adjust. Because the primary patients were the father and two asthmatic children, the following treatment plan was worked out: (1) to control the children's asthma; (2) to relieve the father's symptoms of anxiety; and (3) to begin individual and family counseling.

The first priority was to eliminate the life-threatening aspects of the asthma attacks through medical control.

It must be remembered that stress does not cause disease. It triggers the disease process, and then the provision of appropriate medical care, preferably preventive care, is essential. In this case, the two asthmatic children, Daniel and Michelle, went on round-the-clock theophylline therapy, which reduces the constriction of the bronchioles, the small airways in the lungs. Once they were on the medication, Daniel and Michelle had fewer attacks. But full asthma control was to come only when the family stress was better controlled.

The second step in the treatment plan was to reduce Allan's anxiety. He had started missing days at work, and his boss had warned him he would be fired unless his record improved. To permit this improvement, swift symptomatic relief with a tranquilizer was essential, not only to keep Allan functional at his job and at home, but also to prevent deterioration into a panic or even psychotic reaction.

In prescribing any medication, it is important to consider the benefit/risk ratio, and in this case, putting the patient on Valium seemed eminently the best thing to do. This treatment would buy some time to keep him functioning and would help hold the family together until it was possible to begin personal and marriage counseling.

I was not surprised that Allan at first resisted the idea of taking any medication that might affect his mental state. He was afraid of becoming dependent. This attitude is very common today. It actually represents a healthy change from the approach, some 10 to 15 years ago, when some patients used to come in asking for tranquilizers because some could produce euphoria.

The difference today is that the benzodiazepine tranquilizers produce little or no euphoria. So, when a tranquilizer is indicated, as it was for this patient, I take great pains to explain the reason for taking the drug, and the benefits and risks of its action. Unless patients understand the reason for taking it and its record of safety, they may not take the medicine they need very much.

It is also essential for patients to understand these facts so they'll take the medication properly. I explained to Allan that he needed to start taking the medication right away to get his symptoms under control. His anxiety was upsetting the family, causing conflicts with his wife and provoking asthma in the children. All these results were upsetting him even more. By breaking that cycle, I explained, the medication might help him to relate more effectively to his wife and children. Once Allan understood these points, he consented to take it.

I then questioned him very carefully about any other medicines he might be taking, either over-the-counter or prescription. Any tranquilizers? Medicines to help him sleep? I warned him against taking any other drugs, whether from a drugstore or another doctor, without first checking with me. When a person is taking a tranquilizer, it is *absolutely essential* to avoid any other drug that will amplify its effect.

I also talked with Allan about drinking alcohol. Like most anxious patients, he was using moderate amounts of whiskey and wine to help him fall asleep at night. I explained that a benzodiazepine tranquilizer would be safer and far more effective than alcohol. He would have relief of his symptoms if he took the medication as directed, but while he was taking it, he could not drink as he had before.

Since confusion was part of Allan's problem at the time, I wrote out my instructions for taking the medication. And I added a reminder of *"No alcohol."* I then asked him to repeat my instructions to assure his understanding. That way, I could be pretty certain that he understood exactly how much medicine to take at exactly what time. I also asked him to post the list on the refrigerator or on the mirror over the bathroom sink. Allan and I agreed on a target date a month later to evaluate whether he would discontinue the medication.

During that first month of treatment Allan came to see me once a week. His symptoms were pretty much under control after only about 3 days of drug therapy.

During this trial month of drug therapy, Allan also began a series of nondrug approaches that helped him control his symptoms. First, he substituted decaffeinated coffee for the eight to ten cups of strong, black caffeinated coffee he had been drinking every day. Second, he started to swim every noon. Midday exercise is very important. Allan found that when he worked off some of his tensions by midday exercise, he was not quite so wrung out with fatigue by day's end. He was then able to participate in family affairs rather than merely to collapse on the couch.

That was a good program for the first few weeks. It is important to start with a simple and limited approach that has a good chance of making the patient feel better. If I pile on too much change at the start, I limit the chance of success. For example, I did not at that time even suggest cutting down on smoking. Eventually, Allan did stop smoking, but not until several years later.

At the same time, I was also seeing Rita on a regular basis for counseling. These separate counseling sessions were to prepare a foundation for marriage counseling. When Allan was feeling better, he and his wife started seeing me together.

Family conflict most often results from lack of communication. As mentioned earlier, the issue around which most family arguments revolve is money. The physician's role is to facilitate communication, to help the couple focus realistically on their common expectations. Allan and Rita had to find out if they had any common ground. They had to learn how to talk to each other in a positive way rather than continually tearing at one another.

After Rita and Allan talked about what they expected from their marriage, I had them try out a simple but standard marriage-counseling technique for one week. I asked them to do something nice for each other every day. Each would then try to guess what the other had done. The idea was to focus on something nice rather than to perpetuate the negative focus.

At the same time, they were reexamining their unrealistic marriage expectations. They had spent too much money on their house. Rita was carrying most of the family responsibility and working full time. This is a common family story. It took time for Rita and Allan to achieve some insight and learn how to communicate, and how to modify, their expectations.

I was highly pleased that Allan and Rita chose to hold their marriage together. But more important, so are they and the children. Five years have passed, and they are all well and happily living together.

Allan has been able to work without interruption, and he is far more comfortable with his work and his responsibilities. He uses tranquilizers from time to time when his anxiety symptoms flare up. This prompt usage of medication is very important. He gets his symptoms under control right away to prevent the cycle of stress that affected his family so severely in the past.

The family's general health has also improved. The members have fewer colds and stomach aches, and the children haven't had any asthma attacks for quite some time.

The important principles of care for this family were:

✱ *identification of stress as the central health factor.*

✱ *positive diagnosis of anxiety in the father.*

✱ *medical control of the children's asthma.*

✱ *immediate symptomatic treatment of the father's anxiety.*

✱ *careful instructions on avoidance of alcohol and other drugs that amplify the effects of benzodiazepine tranquilizers.*

* *emphasis to the patient on the importance of medication to control symptoms.*

* *setting a target date for discontinuation of the tranquilizer. The idea is to let the patient know that the drug will not be taken regularly and forever.*

* *adding nondrug approaches as the patient starts feeling better. Eventually, the nondrug approaches became the most important treatment.*

* *periodic short-term use of benzodiazepine tranquilizers whenever symptoms flare up, to prevent the resumption of the cycle of stress in the family.*

This approach has been successful for many people. As a physician, I can't rescue people or solve their problems. But I hope my report of this case shows how a family physician can successfully serve as facilitator and interactor, and as a sounding board to help people solve their problems themselves.

## Depression: "Dark Night of the Soul"

Abraham Lincoln went through recurring bouts of depression that began in young manhood. Nathaniel Hawthorne at one point became so overwhelmed that for 12 years he rarely left his room. "I have made a captive of myself," he wrote Longfellow, "and put me into a dungeon, and now I cannot find the key to let myself out."

Winston Churchill called his depressions "my black dog." Once, he recalled, "for two or three years, the light faded out of the picture. . . . I sat in the House of Commons but black depression settled on me."

While experiencing depression, F. Scott Fitzgerald described it by writing, "In a real dark night of the soul, it is always 3 o'clock in the morning."

Much of their suffering could have been relieved today.

Of all mental illnesses, depression has come to be recognized in recent years as the most common.

Studies by the National Institute of Mental Health reveal that an estimated 8 million Americans are suffering from depression serious enough to require treatment, that 125,000 are hospitalized each year for the condition, and that probably another 200,000 should be hospitalized. These figures, however, may be conservative; some authorities have estimated that the number of depressed people is as high as 15 million.

"A lowering or decrease of functional activity. Absence of cheerfulness or hope: emotional dejection." This is one dictionary definition. But it hardly begins to picture the distressing human experience.

Who are the victims? Almost anyone can be, at any age, in any station in life, male or female.

And, because stress can foment depression, it is no stranger in the lives of many executives, although it is not always recognized early enough as depression.

### A Word about Ordinary "Blues"

Almost all of us, of course, are familiar with the occasional feeling of being "down," "blue," "dejected." At such times, all life may look bleak, nothing is satisfying, and it may be difficult to get oneself to do anything.

Such ordinary episodes have many causes. They are natural, predictable reactions to everyday stress and frustration. Life provides us with many kinds of passing crises that temporarily cloud mood—from a dented fender to a rainy Sunday, from postholiday letdown to excessive work demands and insufficient sleep.

# Depression is now recognized as the most common of all mental illnesses.

Moreover, each of us inevitably encounters major crisis periods bringing sadness, as when a friend dies, an investment goes bad, a child becomes hostile. We can become dejected in the wake of a long, futile spell of work or a sudden stress such as an auto accident.

But, normally, the intensity and duration of dejection are proportionate to the significance of what brought it on. The loss on the one hand of a favorite memento and, on the other hand, of a job are hardly expected to result in the same degree of emotion.

If the blues are ordinary, normal, and proportionate, they disappear spontaneously, are over in a reasonable period, and life becomes normal again.

## The Real Thing: How Serious Can It Be?

Severe depression is something quite different from the ordinary blues. It hangs on; it can be overwhelming, making it difficult, sometimes even impossible, for its victims to function. At the very extreme, it can lead to suicide.

But, short of that, consider a case of severe depression in a 49-year-old executive vice president of a major industrial company.

It infiltrated R.D.'s life over a 3-month period. At first, he simply felt extraordinarily tired. "A terrible tiredness," he called it. He had been entirely well before, and had enjoyed his work very much. But now it became burdensome. He had to put out great effort to do his desk work. Without even fully realizing what he was doing, he found excuses for avoiding his usual business trips.

In another few weeks, he was experiencing generalized aches and pains. He was an excellent squash player but now he stopped playing: he was too tired, too achy, and he felt a mounting fear that he might suffer a heart attack. Day by day, he felt worse and worse. Living through the day became an effort. He found himself not wanting to wake up in the morning. At that time, he felt worst of all.

He had begun to worry about a possible heart attack when he had experienced some shortness of breath. Now lack of breath intensified. So did sleeping difficulty. He could fall asleep all right. But he was up, unable to get back to sleep again, hours before it was time to get up for the day. He was experiencing headaches, very severe. And he felt tight pains in the back of his neck all the time, sometimes spreading behind his eyes.

There was a hospital workup. Many tests were taken. All were negative.

Diagnosis: Depression.

### The Continuing Cloud: Symptoms and Disguises

Significant depression can produce a wide range of physical, emotional, and mental symptoms.

To begin with, there are emotional changes—notably, a depressed mood. Hanging over the victim's head like a heavy shroud is an aura of gloom and sadness. Ability to experience pleasure is diminished or gone. There may be crying spells, often without obvious provocation. There may be anxiety, ranging from feelings of apprehension to outright panic; irritability; feelings of guilt and remorse. And commonly, there is a dramatic decline in self-confidence and self-esteem.

Frequently, there are marked changes in mental state. A victim of depression may experience difficulty in concentrating, poor memory, indecisiveness, and a loss of interest in the work that normally commands attention. Finding life flat and meaningless, he or she may brood about death.

Depression has been called the *great masquerader* because often, despite mood and behavioral changes, physical symptoms seem overriding. Fatigue and slowing of physical and mental energy are prominent. There may also be appe-

Significant depression can produce a wide range of physical, emotional, and mental symptoms.

tite loss and digestive difficulties, heart palpitation, insomnia, headache, reduction or loss of sexual drive, dizziness, and visual disturbances.

Frequently, a victim's concern with physical discomforts may be so great that little attention is paid to the other indications of depression or they may be thought to be the results of the physical symptoms. And, commonly, when medical help is sought, the patient may detail the physical complaints and fail to mention others.

Unless the victim is aware of the importance of the mood and behavioral disturbances, or unless the physician is alert to the possibilities and makes an effort to ferret them out, treatment may be focused—uselessly—on the symptoms instead of—beneficially—on the causes.

Some studies have indicated that the elapsed time from onset of depression to its recognition can range up to 36 months, during which time patients, if they receive any treatment, often may be treated for other illnesses.

One recent study involved 100 consecutive patients seen at the University of Mississippi Medical Center and Jackson Veterans Administration Hospital, who were referred by physicians and found to be depressed. Many had seen physicians on several occasions because of sleep disturbances, had asked for sleeping pills, and, in almost 100 percent of the cases, had received them, though the depression was overlooked.

Many others had been treated with analgesics for aches and pains; some had received antacids; still others had been given antinausea drugs. When carefully interviewed at the Center and the Hospital, they admitted to many other symptoms suggesting depression.


### Causes

What actually brings on depression?

Many investigators believe that some underlying genetic or biological vulnerability is involved, but having this predisposing factor does not mean that the illness is inevitable.

"The situation is somewhat analogous to diabetes," says Frederick K. Goodwin, M.D., distinguished researcher at the National Institute of Mental Health. "Someone who has an inherited vulnerability to diabetes may not get it if that person keeps his or her weight under control. The same is true of depression except that here we're talking about the interaction of psychological and biological factors."

Stress is the major psychological factor in depression.

"Most depressions are brought on by stress events—principally stress due to a loss," says Richard C. Proctor, M.D., professor in the Bowman Gray School of Medicine of Wake Forest University.

Triggering loss can be of many kinds. "You may lose someone you care about very much through death, divorce, or just because that someone has moved to another part of the country," observes Dr. Proctor. "The loss could be more personal. What is more personal than losing your hair, putting on too much weight, or realizing one morning when you look in the mirror that you are not 18 years old or even 38 years old anymore?"

Dr. Proctor continues:

Here are other examples: The esteem in which you may have been held by others might be shattered. This can cause stress, just as can loss of self-esteem or self-confidence. What of loss of your security, or your cherished dream or a symbolic loss, you might ask? Often, it is not so much who is lost, but what is lost and the "what" will vary from one person to another. What is important to one individual may be not as important to another.

Whether you are part of the management structure of a large corporation or running your own business, there can be an unending list of stresses coming from your work. You may feel lonely or develop feelings of inadequacy. Adapting to an unaccustomed social position or a new culture and environment can bring on stress.

If personal values run counter to values in your business, that can precipitate guilt, which in turn is followed by depression and anxiety.

# Stress is the major psychological factor in depression.

## Treating Depression

It may be hard to believe that only 300 years ago in Europe and Great Britain, depression victims were likely to be chained in rat-infested prisons. And in the early days of the United States and for decades thereafter, the depressed and other mentally ill persons were stored in infamous "snake pits" that passed as mental hospitals. Even early in the nineteenth century, some American physicians were using such treatments as purgatives and a "tranquilizing" chair that restrained the patient with leather straps and wooden helmet and looked somewhat like the modern electric chair.

With the development of modern psychiatry, we now have a therapeutic, rather than a punitive, approach to emotional and behavioral disorders, and treatment for depression has become increasingly effective. For the depressions that primarily involve a psychological state with sadness, loss of interest, hopeless feelings, and inability to enjoy, some form of psychotherapy is often helpful. When a depression is severe enough to disturb sleep, inhibit appetite and energy, and interfere with normal functioning, antidepressant medication may be needed. In many cases, a combination of drugs and psychotherapy is successful.

In one study of patients with moderately severe de-

## ARE YOU DEPRESSED?

Everybody feels depressed occasionally. A first question to ask yourself is: "How long has my depressed mood persisted?" If you have been depressed for more than 2 weeks, you may need help. Aaron T. Beck, professor of psychiatry at the University of Pennsylvania School of Medicine, suggests: "When the Monday morning blahs are still around on Friday, or the weekend slump continues through the following week, it's time to suspect something more serious."

Another possible danger signal: You find yourself drinking too much or making regular use of drugs. Both alcoholism and drug abuse can represent efforts to escape the psychological pain of depression.

Still other danger signals include the appearance of physiological disturbances, sleeping difficulty, appetite loss, energy loss, difficulty in concentrating, and anxiety and nervousness, especially early in the morning.

# ELECTROSHOCK: IS IT STILL NECESSARY?

Electroshock therapy, more properly called electro-convulsive therapy (ECT), is very effective for severe depression. For certain patients, particularly some suicidal patients, it may be the only treatment that works. With the increasing availability of antidepressant drugs, ECT is used less often. It is reserved by some psychiatrists for patients, relatively few, who do not respond to drugs. And it is often used, because it works quickly, when, as in the case of a severely suicidal patient, it might be dangerous to wait for an antidepressant drug to work.

With modern techniques, ECT is rapid, painless, and not dangerous. It can produce some temporary memory loss but there has never been any substantiation of old fears of brain damage.

But ECT has been and remains controversial. In the words of Dr. Goodwin of the National Institute of Mental Health: "The controversy is more emotional than scientific, at least in regard to its use in severe depression. For one thing, no one really understands how it works, and we tend to not trust the things that we don't understand. Also, in the days before tranquilizers, it was sometimes used repeatedly to control psychotic and destructive behavior, and, under these conditions—not used today—ECT could conceivably produce a subtle form of brain damage. Finally, it just seems at first glance to be sort of barbaric—giving an electric current to produce a convulsion. But the bottom line is that ECT can dramatically reverse the devastation of severe depression."

pression, drugs and psychotherapy as treatment were compared. The investigators determined that:

Patients who got drugs alone had marked improvement in the physiological symptoms of depression. Sleep, appetite, energy level, and ability to function all returned essentially to normal. But low self-esteem and interpersonal difficulties remained.

With psychotherapy alone, self-esteem and interpersonal relations improved but the physiological symptoms did not.

Patients who received both drugs and psychotherapy improved in both areas.

No matter which treatment or combination of treatments is used, it is even more important than many realize that treatment continue past the point of feeling a little better to the point of assurance that recovery is well on the way. Meanwhile, medications can be lessened in strength and other types of treatment decreased in frequency, until full recovery occurs.

## Drugs for Depression

Many antidepressant agents are available and new ones keep coming. Some examples of those in common use are Tofranil, Elavil, Aventyl, Pertofrane, Norpramin, and Sinequan.

Commonly, antidepressants take about 3 weeks to begin to work and another few weeks to exert their full effects. The drugs are not identical chemically, and a person who does not respond to one may respond to another. All told, about 80 percent of people with major depressions will have a virtually complete remission with one or another of the drugs, according to reports.

Side reactions, when they occur, are usually more annoying than serious. The most common are dryness of the mouth and some constipation. For the first few days of treatment, there may be some sleepiness, and occasionally a patient may feel a bit unusual or peculiar for a brief period. When side reactions are troublesome, a switch may be made to another antidepressant which, in the individual case, may combat the depression with fewer, less bothersome, or no undesirable effects.

There is a type of depressive illness, called *manic* or *bipolar*, in which recurrent bouts of severe depression alternate with episodes of great elation, sometimes manifested in flamboyant speech and action, or feelings of being unable to do anything wrong.

For manic-depressive illness, a relatively new treatment, lithium carbonate, is often effective in preventing recurrences of both the mania and the depression.

## Psychotherapy

Psychotherapy is often a valuable aid to the depressed patient. It may be used to uncover the emotional background of distress and to help change personality and living patterns so that recurrence of depression is less likely.

Although a number of techniques are used in psychotherapy, there are basically two approaches: insight-oriented treatment and behavior-centered treatment.

With insight-oriented therapy, an effort is made to uncover the roots of the patient's emotional problems, to find the emotional factors involved in the depression. The objective is to increase the patient's understanding of his or her own behavior and not solely to attack the symptoms. This therapy suggests that earlier events, even those occurring in childhood, may exert a powerful influence on later behavior.

Behavior-centered psychotherapy, in contrast, is aimed at modifying behavior directly rather than by probing into underlying causes. The goal is to help the depressed person to get rid of old, bad habits and to acquire new responses to stress.

In recent years, group psychotherapy has become common. It is based on recognition that psychological disturbances are often a product of relationships with other persons—and that learning new ways of interacting with others is often best achieved in a group that offers opportunities for such interaction.

## Anxiety, Depression, and the Caffeine Connection

Excessive caffeine intake, not only via coffee and tea but also via cola drinks, hot chocolate, cocoa, chocolate bars, and, as well, caffeine-containing medications, can produce symptoms very much like those of anxiety or depression.

It was John Greden, M.D., then of Walter Reed Army Medical Center, who brought that finding to light several years ago at an American Psychiatric Association meeting, along with some dramatic cases of people who benefited when the problem was recognized.

One, a young nurse married to an army physician, sought medical help because of several weeks of light-headedness, tremulousness, breathlessness, headache, and irregular heartbeat. After examination showed no physical basis, she was referred to a psychiatric outpatient clinic with a diagnosis of anxiety.

But, refusing to accept that diagnosis, the young nurse was the first to suspect the possible cause, and in about 10 days she managed to link her symptoms to coffee consumption. She had started making coffee by a different method that she found superior and so had been drinking 10 to 12 cups a day. Her symptoms disappeared within 36 hours after she stopped drinking coffee. She was later challenged with caffeine twice, and each time the symptoms returned, only to disappear when the caffeine was eliminated.

Another case involved a 37-year-old military officer referred for psychiatric help after a 2-year history of chronic anxiety. His symptoms occurred almost daily and included dizziness, tremulousness, apprehension about job performance, restlessness, frequent diarrhea, and persistent sleep problems. Medical examination provided no explanation. Tranquilizers had little effect.

Finally, it was discovered that he drank 8 to 14 cups of coffee a day and often drank hot cocoa at bedtime. He liked only cola soft drinks and often drank 3 or 4 a day. He was incredulous at the idea that a caffeine reaction might be causing his problems and unwilling at first to cut down on coffee, cocoa, and colas. But he finally gave in. A few weeks later, he reported marked improvement.

Greden's finding that large amounts of caffeine can produce symptoms mimicking those of chronic anxiety was soon confirmed by other investigators.

## The Anxiety Dose

Individual sensitivity to caffeine, as to almost anything else, varies. For some people, however, Greden found that as little as 250 milligrams a day may be enough to produce symptoms similar to those of chronic anxiety. Among them are

# Individual sensitivity to caffeine varies.

restlessness, irritability, headache, racing pulse, flushing, lethargy, nausea, vomiting, diarrhea, and chest pain.

Many people exceed an intake of 250 milligrams almost daily. For example, consume 3 cups of coffee, 2 caffeine-containing headache tablets, and a caffeine-containing cola drink—all of which you might do in a morning—and you've taken in, not 250, but 500, milligrams of caffeine.

In surveys among general populations, including such subgroups as housewives and medical students, 20 to 30 percent of respondents have been found to consume more than 500 to 600 milligrams of caffeine daily.

## *Caffeine, Depression, and Fatigue*

Two years after his report on caffeine and anxiety, Greden and a group of associates reported on another study that took the caffeine story a potentially important step further.

They administered a questionnaire to eighty-three psychiatric patients as they were hospitalized at the University of Michigan Medical Center and the Ann Arbor Veterans Administration Hospital. The questionnaire covered types and amounts of caffeine consumed, self-observed effects of caffeine use, history of anxiety symptoms, and other psychiatric problems. The researchers also tested the patients for anxiety and depression.

Based on their caffeine intake, the patients were divided into three groups: "low" consumers who took in less than 250 milligrams per day; "moderate" ones who consumed 250 to 749 milligrams daily; and "high" consumers whose intake exceeded 750 milligrams. Even with the arbitrarily set high level of 750 milligrams or more for high consumers, 22 percent of the patients fell into that category; 42 percent were moderate, and 36 percent were low consumers.

A significantly greater number of the highest consumers also reported getting in a state of tension over personal concerns, thinking that difficulties were piling up, feeling like crying, and feeling blue. Inversely, a much smaller percentage of the high consumers reported feeling pleasant, rested, happy, or content.

As caffeine intake rose, anxiety symptoms increased and

## CAFFEINE CONTENT OF FOODS AND DRUGS

Coffee (6 oz):
| | |
|---|---|
| Automatic drip | 181 mg |
| Automatic perk | 125 mg |
| Instant | 54 mg |

Soft Drinks (12 oz):
| | |
|---|---|
| Mountain Dew | 54 mg |
| Mellow Yellow | 51 mg |
| Dr. Pepper | 38 mg |
| Pepsi-Cola | 38 mg |
| Coca-Cola | 33 mg |
| Tab | 32 mg |
| RC Cola | 26 mg |

Tea (6 oz):
| | |
|---|---|
| Iced tea | 69 mg |

Tea brand—according to length of steeping time:

| | Weak | Medium | Strong |
|---|---|---|---|
| Red Rose | 45 mg | 62 mg | 90 mg |
| Tetley | 18 mg | 48 mg | 70 mg |
| English Breakfast | 26 mg | 78 mg | 107 mg |

Drugs:
| | |
|---|---|
| Dexatrim capsules (Thompson) | 200 mg/tablet |
| Nodōz tablets (Bristol-Myers) | 100 mg/tablet |
| Anacin (Whitehall) | 32.5 mg/tablet |
| Midol (Glenbrook) | 32.4 mg/tablet |
| Coricidin (Schering) | 30 mg/tablet |

Cocoa:
| | |
|---|---|
| Chocolate candy (2 oz) | 45 mg |
| Baking chocolate (1 oz) | 45 mg |
| South American (5 oz) | 42 mg |
| Milk chocolate candy (2 oz) | 12 mg |
| African (6 oz) | 5 mg |

SOURCE: "The Health Effects of Caffeine," a report by the American Council on Science and Health.

feelings of calmness decreased. Despite their symptoms, few heavy consumers associated their problems with caffeine. In fact, some claimed that coffee or tea made them less depressed.

A much larger percentage of high consumers reported frequent use of tranquilizers. And one-half the heavy consumers rated very high on a standard depression scale, their scores suggesting severe depression.

Considering sources of caffeine consumption, the researchers found that the high consumers averaged 75 percent of their intake from coffee, 10 to 15 percent from tea, 5 to 10 percent from cola drinks, and 5 to 10 percent from medications. Caffeine intake usually started by age 15 for the highest consumers and somewhat later for the others, suggesting that the caffeine syndrome may take years to develop.

The Michigan researchers were not surprised at the high incidence of anxiety symptoms among high caffeine consumers. Not only is the drug a nervous system stimulant; it also increases body output of the hormone norepinephrine, which in excess is known to contribute to anxiety.

What was surprising was the high incidence of depression among the heavy consumers. One possible explanation is that some people may self-medicate with caffeine upon becoming depressed. But it is also possible that chronic high caffeine ingestion helps trigger depressive symptoms in some people. Some highly complex biological mechanisms that may be affected by the drug are under investigation.

Perhaps, Dr. Greden suggests, physicians treating high caffeine consumers for anxiety or depression should ask them to cut down their intake for a week or so and see what happens.

That, of course, is something any victim of anxiety, depression, or fatigue, is privileged to try without outside instructions.

# STRESS AND THE WOMAN EXECUTIVE

**O**ne of the most significant and profound changes in American society in this century is the growing participation of women in roles once considered almost exclusively those of men.

The number of women who work has about doubled in just a few decades. The typical working woman, moreover, is married and a mother. "The traditional family of Western nostalgia is disappearing," notes Phyllis Moen, professor of human development and family studies at Cornell University. She reports:*

> The American family stereotype of a father working while the mother stays home to raise two children depicts only 7 percent of all U.S. families; only 15 percent are families in which the father is the sole wage earner.
>
> We're experiencing the most dramatic period of change in the history of American women. An unprecedented number of women, including mothers, are now part of the labor force.

In 1980, 57 percent of all mothers were working, compared with 30 percent in 1960 and 9 percent in 1940. Nearly half of all American children had working mothers in 1980; one-quarter of those children were younger than 6 years old.

"The impact of women working outside the home is a positive force," believes Professor Moen, "transforming the nature of the household as well as the workplace."

* Phyllis Moen, Report from New York State College of Human Ecology, Cornell University, May 6, 1981.

## The typical working woman is married and a mother.

## The Woman Executive's Special Challenges

Part of the transformation in the workplace lies in the slow but steady acceptance of women and recognition of their place in management in recent years.

There were, in 1969, some 1.3 million women managers, all told, in industry, government, and education, and self-employed as business owners. In 1979, according to the U.S. Department of Labor, the number had increased to 2.6 million. Even so, in that year, women held only one-fourth of all managerial jobs.

Nearly 602,000 women were employed as managers and officials in companies reporting to the Equal Employment Opportunity Commission in 1978. They represented 17 percent of all executives in those companies in which women made up 40 percent of the total work force.

And in 1977, the last year for which figures have been compiled by the Department of Labor, women managers who worked full-time year round had a median income of only 55 percent of that earned by men in management.

### Breaking In

Women executives, of course, encounter many of the same stressful problems that men do. They may experience quite a few others as well.

As women have begun to take their place in increasing numbers in American offices, no longer only as clerical helpers but also as professional colleagues and executives, it has seemed to many men that the office is no longer what it once was, a kind of male club.

Men have had to make adjustments. No longer appropriate are some of the old, easy ways of relating among men—the jokes and bantering. To some men, having a woman boss has loomed as awkward, even to some extent threatening.

On the other hand, for women, the office may still seem to be a male club, strange and hostile.

In a recent report dealing with occupational stress, Dr. Tobias Brocher of the Menninger Center for Applied Behavioral Sciences talked of "the growing number of female executives in an all-male world who are in isolated positions, surrounded by men who are either courteous in a stereotyped but phony way, or openly hostile and derogative in their competition."

"Ulcers, gastrointestinal disorders, and emotional distress prevail in these women as a result of common male prejudice," Dr. Brocher remarked.

Recently, too, Dr. Leon J. Warshaw, also a specialist in occupational health, observed:

In part, the woman worker's problems reflect the fact that she is a newcomer. . . . As a colleague put it, "She doesn't know how to behave in that male locker room and the men don't quite know how to react to her presence."

The aggressiveness that the woman has to muster to enter this domain and her justified resentment in instances when she had to be better qualified and accept lower pay to win the job are sometimes translated into an abrasiveness that makes her hard to take.

Some studies have suggested that a woman who gains a leadership position can expect, almost as a matter of course, to meet resistance from the staff—and the resistance may

# Nearly half of all American children had working mothers in 1980.

> # To some men, having a woman boss has loomed as awkward, and to some, even threatening.

not be confined to men only. Accustomed to having a male leader, both male and female workers may feel that they cannot be properly represented by a woman. They may assume that the man to whom she reports may be the real authority, threatening the integrity of the group.

Some men in the group may also make some effort to undermine a woman executive's authority by covertly performing functions that should be hers and by treating her not as a superior but as an equal.

### Stereotypical Attitudes

Despite the gains of women in recent years, there still remain, even if a little less widespread, some stereotypical attitudes which hamper the full utilization of women in management.

Some employers hold the view that it does not pay to train or promote women, especially in professional or managerial positions, because they will marry and leave the company, thus causing an investment loss to the employer.

Yet, this allegation was refuted in a study by the Aetna Life Insurance Company as far back as 1973. It showed that women in technical, supervisory, and managerial positions turned over at the rate of 8.5 percent a year, while men in comparable jobs turned over at a 9.0 percent rate. Absence rates were found to be identical for men and women, which, the U.S. Department of Labor points out, is also consistent with the national data.

Still, it is often argued that if women in management fail to move ahead as far and as fast as men even when both have equal credentials, such as an M.B.A. degree, slower advancement is to be expected, for women bear the brunt of family duties. They are more likely to work only part-time for some period in their careers and to turn down assignments requiring travel and long hours because of child-rearing responsibilities.

A study shedding light on these questions was conducted by Columbia University's Center for Research in Career Development. It considered forty men and forty women graduates of the 1969 through 1972 classes at Columbia's Graduate School of Business, all carefully selected so they had comparable social, economic, and academic backgrounds.

The study found that among the women earning over $50,000, some 65 percent were married, as compared with about 60 percent of those earning less than $50,000 (and about 75 percent of the men in the group). Moreover, two-thirds of the married women earning over $50,000 had children.

Mary Anne Devanna, research coordinator at the Columbia center and the author of the study, says: "There isn't any overwhelming indication that women have to give up human roles to succeed." Family concerns, she adds, "aren't what is keeping women from getting ahead."

Liz Roman Gallese of the *Wall Street Journal* has reported on a little study of her own carried out over several months early in 1981. She checked with some fifty professionals and managerial women, all of whom had earned M.B.A. degrees 5 to 8 years before. There emerged from her data much the same pattern found in the Columbia study. She summarizes:*

> Of the eighteen who I feel are the most "ambitious," as defined by their progress so far and the decisions they've already made about their careers—a decision to relocate, for example, or to accept a job considered risky but potentially lucrative, twelve are married. Of the twelve who are married, eight have at least one child. One has three.

Nor, Gallese points out, are researchers and consultants entirely surprised by such findings even though it is widely assumed that successful women are likely to be single or divorced. She notes that a consulting firm, Pioneer Management, Inc., of Mercer Island, Washington, which works with

*"Manager's Journal," *Wall Street Journal*, May 4, 1981.

companies trying to advance women, finds that women executives today are increasingly taking supposed "male attitudes" toward their careers.

Some experts think that successful women are able to coordinate careers and families because they are so highly motivated that they believe they can.

Basing her judgment on what she found, Gallese is convinced that such women manage because of certain characteristics. She reports.:

> These characteristics are even more noteworthy because they are specifically lacking in a group of about two dozen women in my sample who are clearly not "ambitious" or who are ambivalent about their careers.
>
> First, the women whom I consider "ambitious" have determined without a doubt that they will work full-time for all of their adult lives.
>
> Second, they understand the realities of building full-fledged careers today. They recognize, for example, that it is difficult to find good part-time work and that it is sometimes necessary to relocate.
>
> Those with children hire someone to care for them and to handle virtually all household tasks—often a person who lives in their homes. And these successful women aren't afraid to demand that their husbands meet them halfway when it comes to decisions about both careers.

## STEREOTYPES OF THE WOMAN EXECUTIVE

Unlike men, women who strive do not automatically get community approval, spouse appreciation, and peer-group support. They are accorded just the opposite, suggests S. P. Hersh, M.D., in his book *The Executive Parent*. He writes:*

"When executive women are overtly aggressive in their pursuit of excellence and/or success, they quickly become aware of uneasiness, guardedness, and disapproval in others. Women executives are clearly more hard put to find the sources of emotional sustenance that assist *everyone* in life, whether the stresses they deal with are ordinary or great.

"They are constantly drained of energy by conflicting demands, double messages, and opposing expectations. To cope,

* S. P. Hersh, *The Executive Parent*, Sovereign Books, 1979.

they mobilize styles of behavior, "marks," and other defenses. The struggles to mobilize these defenses can produce subclinical depressions that evolve into chronic mood states of dissatisfaction and feelings of isolation.

"In their attempts to cover these states, women executives not infrequently resort to increased activity or the actual assumption of one of the expected caricature roles, such as the 'aggressive, castrating bitch,' the 'deceptively helpless, manipulative maneuverer,' or the 'seductive, moody, loyalty-changing climber.'"

Yet, Hersh points out, women who cope successfully with "these incredibly challenging stresses" do exist. They are able to remain in touch with themselves; they deal with the system without letting it distort their basic values and without making the kinds of accommodations that lead to chronic repressed anger.

There are other sources of stress on women executives, including what Hersh terms "the reality that if they choose to be executives *and* have husbands and children, they take up a struggle which puts them in the category of 'superfemale,' 'supermomma,' and 'superwoman.'"

The energy required of such women is extraordinary, says Hersh:

"They have little time for insight and introspection as they superhumanly switch roles from executive to homemaker (another form of executive), to wife, mother, and lover. Usually, a woman handles this struggle by creating stages in her life (mother stage, work stage, and many other variations on this theme) or by compartmentalizing her activities while relying heavily on housekeepers and relatives to fill in for her at home."

Ulcers, gastrointestinal disorders, and emotional distress prevailing in these women are a result of common male prejudice.

Why, then, do so many people—women and men alike—continue to assume that family responsibilities must necessarily interfere with women's careers? Gallese answers:

> Perhaps because the assumption is so convenient. It is convenient for male managers who feel uneasy about promoting women. It is easier, for example, to rationalize that a woman will get pregnant and leave than it is to admit that you can't perceive women supervising men.
>
> The assumption is also convenient for women who fail to take charge of careers that have become routine, as careers often do. The possibility of quitting to care for the children gives such women an easy out.
>
> But, [Gallese concludes] a growing proportion of the best young managerial talent is female. Some 20 percent to 50 percent of students graduating from professional schools today are women, up from less than 5 percent a decade ago. If companies, and women themselves, are to make the best use of this talent, they will have to stop hiding behind the excuse that it can't be done because of women's family duties. The good news is that there is plenty of evidence that women can combine careers and family.

# THE DEPRESSIVE REACTIONS OF SOME WOMEN EXECUTIVES

We see depressive reactions among some women executives. I have some hypotheses about why.

I have a feeling that women have long been socialized to be affiliative, to be warm.

And when they enter the corporate world, they are in a world where affiliation is controlled and dangerous—or, perhaps a better way of putting it, where affiliation is problematic.

It can be a world in which, to be effective, you must be able to use people, and when necessary, say goodbye to people. To receive too much from other people—to have your needs for warmth and togetherness met can be dangerous.

My guess is that much of the depression we may see in women in management comes when, socialized to one role—of affiliation and warmth—they find themselves in a world in which warmth is rarely given and rarely meant sincerely, where it becomes a tool.

On top of that, there is the problem that corporations often don't know quite what to do with women. They have value systems that are not those of women, and they may not really like the intrusion.

So not only does a woman in management have to adjust to a different emotional role, but she is at best in an indifferent and sometimes even basically hostile environment.

And in our society, a relationship between intimacy and sexuality whenever there is a heterosexual pair is a burden.

Women as a rule tend to compete with other women in terms of the socialization process. Men tend to form close affiliative relationships with men. But as soon as men and women become intimate, the sexual element almost invariably arises.

So a woman is somewhat deprived of the emotional closeness and camaraderie men develop. And she is shut out of the old-boy network.

Dr. Herbert Krauss, Consulting Psychologist
Executive Health Examiners

## Conflicts

Women are in the work force to stay—not only to help support their families but also to achieve personal satisfaction, according to a recent national survey. At the same time, however, the survey showed that working mothers bear particular pressures that have impact on their ability to build their careers and carry out their family duties to their satisfaction.

The study, called "Families at Work: Strengths and Strains," was conducted by Louis Harris & Associates under the sponsorship of General Mills. Its respondents included 1503 adult family members, 235 teenagers in those families, 104 business executives, 56 labor leaders, 49 so-called family traditionalists whose names were provided by conservative groups, and 52 feminists whose names were supplied by women's rights organizations.

According to the survey, a majority (52 percent) of family members believe that the trend toward both husband and wife working outside the home has negative effects on families.

"The reason most often cited for this," reported Louis Harris, president of the research organization involved, "is that 'children need stronger parental guidance, supervision and discipline' than can be given when both parents work."

# A woman is somewhat deprived of the emotional closeness and camaraderie men develop.

On the other hand, most of the respondent feminists and a majority of the working women believe that when both parents work, there are positive or no effects at all on families. Among the positive effects mentioned were fulfillment of working women, increased financial security, improved family communications, and independence for children.

All groups in the survey agreed with the statement, "When both parents work, children have to become more self-reliant and independent."

Most of the women working outside the home—more than 5 of every 10 living in families—are married and the majority have children under the age of 18. Of all these women, 58 percent said they would prefer to continue working even if there were no economic need, 28 percent said no; and 14 percent expressed no opinion.

But in what Louis Harris called "a somewhat more surprising finding," the number of women now working who would, in the absence of need, prefer part-time employment was $2\frac{1}{2}$ times larger than the number of those who would prefer full-time. And an even greater number of women currently in executive managerial or professional jobs indicated a preference for part-time employment (51 percent) over full-time (19 percent).

"Interesting part-time work opportunities might relieve the tension between work and family responsibilities that many working women are clearly experiencing," Harris said.

Respondents could agree on no single solution to conflicting demands of work and family responsibilities, but the survey did find what Harris described as "a clear call for mutual consideration." In other words, there was a demand for business to consider ways to accommodate family needs just as families consider ways to meet terms imposed by the workplace.

"I'd like to say this to business," Harris remarked. "You're going to be in the bull's-eye for the next three or four years to meet these conditions."

Among the most discussed policies, Harris noted, is part-time work with full benefits, which 42 percent of family members, 49 percent of working women, and 66 percent of women planning to work felt would help them and their families significantly. Of the working mothers, 53 percent said they thought that employees should have the right to resume work at the same pay and seniority after a personal leave of absence.

At a press conference at which results of the surveys were announced, H. Brewster Atwater, Jr., president and chief executive officer of General Mills, the survey sponsor, was asked what his company was doing to ease employees' conflicts between work and family duties.

"We are wrestling right now," he replied, "with what to do when the spouse of a married employee gets a job offer in another city. This is going to be happening more often in the face of the fact that 50 percent of the business school graduates of the future will be women." He noted, too, that the largest single change at General Mills over the last decade was the increase in part-time work. "If you work more than 3 days a week," he said, "you qualify for full-time benefits."

The difficulties encountered when juggling a busy career with a demanding home life can take a heavy toll, however.

M.T., a 28-year-old account executive for a large Wall Street brokerage firm, is married to a busy lawyer. They both have full days professionally that leave them tired at the end of the day. They also have a 3-year-old child who requires attention from both of them evenings and weekends.

For the past year, there has been increasing friction concerning M.T.'s domestic role. Although they employed a daytime baby-sitter, the responsibility of preparing dinner and keeping the apartment clean had routinely been accepted by M.T., while her husband spent time with their son. They rarely had an evening out, since they felt the obligation to stay home at night. M.T. increasingly resented this aspect of her domestic role, and her feelings led to frequent disagreements that resulted in marital discord and the onset of frequent tension headaches.

# Juggling a busy career with a demanding home life can take a heavy toll.

During her company-sponsored physical examination, the physician noted that M.T. complained of fatigue, yet had trouble sleeping at night. The EHE doctor asked M.T. to return with her husband for an appointment with the staff psychologist. Subsequently, they were advised about the importance of sharing at home; taking turns with meal preparation and playing with their child; getting a baby-sitter 2 nights a week to allow an evening out with each other and/or friends; and getting away with the entire family on weekends to avoid the necessity of domestic preparations. They were also convinced by the psychologist that their combined professional income was substantial enough to hire a regular housekeeper to handle the routine cleaning and upkeep of the apartment. In addition, with the help of a learned relaxation response, M.T. is sleeping better and has far fewer headaches.

If both spouses are busy executives, they must work together in a spirit of sharing and mutual cooperation and remember not to be pennywise and pound-foolish. Investing wisely in domestic help provides vital time for important family relationships to develop.

## Working Women and Heart Disease

The number of women working full-time outside the home has multiplied in the past few years. By entering the 9-to-5 rat race, have women increased their risk of developing coronary heart disease (CHD) over what it would have been had they remained housewives?

Generally no, according to a study by Drs. Suzanne Haynes and Manning Feinleib of the National Institutes of

Health's Heart, Lung and Blood Institute Epidemiology Branch.* The 8-year study, using data from the Framingham Heart Study (which began in 1948), concluded that working women did not have significantly higher incidence rates of CHD than housewives. However, some exceptions were found when women were placed in specific occupational and marital categories.

Beginning in 1965, a 300-item psychosocial questionnaire was given to 1319 participants (352 housewives, 387 working women, and 580 men). The questionnaire assessed employment and occupational status, personality type, situational stress, reactions to anger, sociocultural mobility, and family responsibilities. The participants were aged 45 to 64 and were free from coronary heart disease at the start of the study. Occupations were classified in three categories: white-collar, clerical, and blue-collar.

A working woman was defined as one who had worked outside the home for more than half her adult life. Regardless of employment status (currently employed, unemployed, retired), women reported more symptoms of emotional stress than men. In addition, working women experienced more job mobility than men, more daily stress, and more marital dissatisfaction than housewives or men. All these differences were statistically significant.

Although the overall data indicate that working women did not experience statistically different incidence rates of CHD than housewives (7.8 versus 5.4 percent), women in clerical occupations had nearly double the incidence of CHD (10.6 percent) than housewives had. CHD rates were also higher among working women who were, or had been, married, especially for those who had raised three or more children.

The study results indicate that women in clerical positions (secretaries, stenographers, bank clerks, bookkeepers, and sales personnel) are at a higher risk of developing coronary heart disease than other women. The risk increases with family responsibilities (that is, having children), and is greater (21.3 percent) if a woman in a clerical occupation has children and is married to a man doing blue-collar work.

*American Journal of Public Health, vol. 70, no. 2, February 1980.

The most significant predictors of CHD among women in clerical occupations were suppressed hostility, having a nonsupportive boss, and lack of job mobility (staying in the same job for a long time).

Previously, it was thought that a man's lifespan was shorter than a woman's because of the man's occupation. Researchers were fearful that with more and more women entering the work force, the incidence of chronic disease such as CHD in these women would begin to show the same mortality statistics as for men.

Dr. Haynes noted that "the Framingham data show that employment of women, in itself, is not related to an increased risk of coronary heart disease. In fact, the women who were employed the longest period of time—the single working women—had the lowest rate of CHD."

## SOME SIMILAR STRESSES FOR WOMEN DOCTORS

The renowned *New England Journal of Medicine* published an editorial, "Women in Medicine: Beyond Prejudice," by Marcia Angell, M.D., in May of 1981. Here are some excerpts from it.

Whatever our viewpoint, I think we can agree on one thing about women in medicine: the average woman physician, that is, the woman who has children, must make major compromises in her profession, in her home, or in both. During her thirties, the period of life when career advancement is most rapid, she carries two sets of serious and time-consuming responsibilities—one to her profession and one to her children.

That both are serious and time-consuming is attested to by the fact that so many men devote themselves exclusively to the first and so many of their wives exclusively to the second. The heart of the dilemma for the woman physician lies in responsibility to oversee the development of her children.

Investing wisely in domestic help provides vital time for important family relationships to develop.

> # Whether employed, unemployed, or retired, women reported more symptoms of emotional stress than men.

If this is important (and few parents think that it isn't) then she inevitably has doubts about the course she has chosen and the priorities it implies. In doing one job well, may she not be doing another, possibly more important job, poorly? A solution is to forfeit professional advancement in return for time—that is, to enter "soft" specialties, look for relatively leisurely or part-time residencies, take salaried positions in clinics or health maintenance organizations, and stay in the lower echelons of academic and organized medicine.

How do her male colleagues see this? Incredibly, many of them choose to see this rather grim and highly responsible series of trade-offs as frivolous or as evidence of incompetence.

For those women who wish to play an active part in raising their children, I believe that there should be a restructuring of medicine in ways that recognize the special needs of the family and the extraordinary efforts that women physicians now make. It is often argued that since the demanding nature of medicine is well known, women should either stay out of it or go into it wholeheartedly, without complaints. This argument, which can be used to justify nearly any long-standing inequity or impropriety, suggests that the structure of medicine is immutable. It isn't.

Part-time work, time out for having and raising a family, and a smooth reentry into medicine could, with only modest ingenuity, be incorporated into the structure of medical training and academic medicine. Choosing such pathways of requiring each woman to blaze her own trail is, at best, clumsy and wasteful of effort. It is also demoralizing.

Women are in medicine to stay. When we force them to choose between their profession and raising their children, rather than providing part-time options and reentry programs, we run two risks. The first, and I think the greater, is that they will choose their profession (such is the status of medicine).

Many authorities see the weakening of the family as a serious threat to our society, and I share their view.

Certainly a strong case can be made that we suffer more from lack of parenting than from lack of doctoring. To the extent that women physicians work part-time in order to raise their children, then, they are performing a highly useful function for all of us.

The other risk is that professional compromises will become a way of life for women even when such compromises are no longer necessary. Women can expect to have about 25 years of professional life after their children are in school. If they have taken time to raise their children, they may find it prohibitively difficult to reenter medicine fully. They may instead continue in a type of practice that doesn't stretch their talents. This is the real inefficiency of women in medicine: talented physicians reluctantly spending their entire professional lives on the fringe.

Our challenge is to adjust to the reality of women's lives instead of denying it, so that they can be better mothers and better doctors.

# COPING EFFECTIVELY

A poem called "The Shoelace," written by Charles Bukowski, contains these lines:

> It's not the large things that
> send a man to the
> madhouse . . .
> not the death of his love
> but a shoelace that snaps
> with no time left. . . .

But why? How come so much impact, conceivably, from a minor nuisance?

Dr. Richard S. Lazarus, a distinguished University of California stress researcher, likes to refer to those lines from "The Shoelace" to make a point: When people get upset over what appear to be trivialities, it's because, for them, the trivial symbolizes something of great import.

When the shoelace breaks, the psychological stress, Lazarus points out, can stem from the implication that you are unable to control your own life, that you are helpless in the face of stupid trivialities, "or, even worse, that such things happen because of your own inadequacies in the first place."

But there is another, more broadly significant, point to be made: Stress is neither good nor bad in itself. The effects of stress are not determined by stress itself, but by how we view and handle the stress, by how we appraise and adapt to an event.

We either handle it properly or let its negative effects get the better of us and we suffer distress.

## Tuning In

To make stress work for you instead of against you, a first vital step may be to recognize that you are overly stressed,

# The effects of stress are determined by how we view and handle the stress, by how we appraise and adapt to an event.

possibly distressed, in one way or another. The recognition process may seem, at first glance, to be unnecessary. Yet our experience at Executive Health Examiners is that executives, like a lot of other people, often tune their bodies to tune out the fact that they are miserable. They keep going on automatic pilot.

Our experience, too, is that while there are a substantial number of valuable techniques for combating stress, the starting point for effective use of one or more of them almost has to be your own recognition that stress is getting to you.

"The first line of coping is self-awareness," emphasizes Allen Collins, M.D., a psychiatric consultant for Executive Health Examiners. "The first thing is to be aware, if it's so, that every day you get up there is a knot in your stomach, or you can't sleep at night and toss and turn and get up at 5 in the morning, or you have diarrhea 4 days a week, or you have a rash on your body and your doctor has told you that it's probably a matter of nerves, or you have headaches, or an ulcer which isn't resolving—this means something. The first line is awareness, and then an effort to figure out what is going on. A lot of people have excellent capacities for figuring out what is going on and even what to do about it. I don't think you need a psychiatrist to do that, a lot of the time."

To become fully aware of the how and when of your own possible stress, you might want to monitor physiological and psychological tension signals for a day or two. For example, every hour or so, you might check on your physical and mental state for a few minutes. Is your heartbeat rapid? Are your muscles tense? Is your stomach tight, or do you feel nauseated? Are you forgetting things? Do you feel as though you are about to explode?

If these are your particular responses to stress, you should be aware of them.

## Ten Stress Signals You Should Heed

* *Are you finding yourself restless and seemingly unable to relax?*

* *Are you irritable and given to anger if things don't go your way?*

* *Do you have periods of prolonged or excessive fatigue?*

* *Do you have concentration difficulty?*

* *Have you lost interest in your usual recreational activities?*

* *Are you worried about things that worry can't help?*

* *Are you working excessively even if not entirely effectively?*

* *Are you taking more and more work home?*

* *Are you smoking more? Drinking more?*

* *Do you suspect now and again that you are losing, or have lost, perspective on what's really important in job and family areas, and maybe in life?*

### Listening to the Organs*

One area that we can often utilize in helping to understand some of our pressures and problems is what I refer to as "organ language." Our "not conscious" (I prefer this term rather than "unconscious" or "subconscious") frequently gives messages and clues to underlying problems and pressures. One can get these clues by "listening to the organs": What do they tell us about our problems?

We all have feelings—good and bad—but we are more inclined to express and show our good feelings and not show our bad ones. Experience shows that when body organ disturbances appear as a result of emotional prob-

* Richard Proctor, M.D., Bowman Gray School of Medicine, Wake Forest University

lems, the body area has some genetic or hereditary tendency toward selecting that organ to signal emotional problems.

Sometimes the coincidence of organ selection is rather dramatic.

A person with nausea and vomiting can have something that he can't stomach or is making him sick to his stomach.

If you have difficulty breathing, you may feel smothered by wife, parents, children, job, or something else.

Visual complaints may be associated with something you don't want to see.

Diarrhea is often due to suppressed hostility, and it is a way to get back at the world.

Skin rashes and eruptions often result from dissatisfaction with the environment for that part of the body which is most exposed to the environment.

Chronic headache may be due to difficulty in figuring out a solution to a problem. The head is what we use to "figure."

Listen to what your body tells you. Often it will help you quickly understand some of the underlying problems and pressures of your life.


## The Competent Copers

People differ in their ability to cope with stress-producing situations. What distinguishes the more successful copers from the less successful ones?

In trying to find out, John M. Rhoads, professor of psychiatry at Duke University School of Medicine, carried out an interesting study with fifteen men he knew personally to be "effective, successful, and physically and mentally healthy." The group included corporate vice presidents and several physicians, lawyers, and academics. All had a work week of at least 60 hours.

The subjects completed a questionnaire on lifestyle, attitude toward work, and personality. Results were compared with an earlier study of fifteen professionals who worked equally long hours but who had developed a syndrome of "overwork" characterized by exhaustion states mimicking serious physical illness.

"Long hours of work," Dr. Rhoads determined, "are not what make one ill. If the work is enjoyed and provides a reasonable amount of freedom of time and judgment away from immediate supervision, there is no good reason for an individual to become ill. Linked to the work situation are personality factors that enable the individual to cope.

"Perhaps the most striking" of these personality features, Rhoads reports, "is the ability to postpone thinking about problems until it is appropriate to deal with them."

All the healthy, successful subjects had this ability. In contrast, the overworked men "were never free of ruminating or of being obsessed about work problems, often to the point that it interfered with the ability to do anything else," Rhoads found.

Although the overworked were in jobs giving them some freedom and independence, they could not tell when they were working so hard that they had gone beyond their endurance. As their productivity diminished through exhaustion, they lengthened their already-long workday to try to compensate.

In contrast, the healthy men were able to spot fatigue. Most responded by quitting work early or taking time off within a week. They differed from the overworked in other important ways: they avoided stimulants, tranquilizers, alcohol, and tobacco abuse; they scheduled and enjoyed vacations; they had stable family situations; they had the ability to form and maintain friendships.

Almost to a man—fourteen of the fifteen—the healthy subjects engaged in regular physical exercise; the overworked men were, almost to a man, sedentary.

The healthy subjects, Rhoads found, also were more likely to have interests outside their work and had a high degree of altruism as reflected by their charitable contribu-

The healthy subjects engaged in regular physical exercise, while the overworked men were sedentary.

tions. They also had what Dr. Rhoads called a "crucial" attribute: a sense of humor and ability to laugh at themselves, while the overworked subjects were notable for their lack of humor.

Although many people utilize the variety of relaxation techniques described in Chapter 10, there are other, less structured pastimes that may be equally effective in helping you slow down and relax. Some of the more common diversions noted by the clients of Executive Health Examiners are reading, listening to music, gardening, painting, sculpturing. There is something for everyone. For example, one of our patients, R.P., is the very successful president of an international conglomerate. As you can imagine, the stress and tension of supervising profit centers worldwide are imposing. However, this individual copes very effectively with his demanding schedule. As well as exercising moderately, he raises exotic orchids, and each evening after returning home, he retreats to his greenhouse for 30 to 45 minutes to care for and enjoy his flowers, a pastime that he finds relaxing and which totally removes him from the stress of his professional life.

In addition to specific relaxation aids, however, do not lose sight of the essential need for *regular vacations* and a sufficient amount of *sleep.* Six hours is a minimum, and you probably need more.

## *Other Attributes of Competent Copers*

Out of other studies of executives successful in coping with stress has come a conviction among some experts that many such executives have in common an awareness of the stress potential in a situation, sensitivity to their own reactions, and capacity to find appropriate responses.

Commonly, the studies suggest, the competent copers analyze stress-producing situations and decide on what is worth worrying about and what is not.

Rather than carry the entire load, they make a point of delegating responsibility, and they may delegate more and more tasks when tension starts to build.

They set priorities and establish goals to achieve the most important objectives.

# Competent copers analyze stress-producing situations and decide on what is worth worrying about and what is not.

They are realistic about perfection—when it is achievable and when not.

When tension begins to build, they talk. They talk with others on the job; they may even have "bitching" sessions with peers; and they commonly talk things through with their spouses. They blow off steam.

Sensitive to their own responses to stress and aware that excessive responses can land them on a frustrating and less-than-full-productive merry-go-round, they are given to taking a break—withdrawing physically from the situation for a while—when that makes sense.

As much as possible, they try to foresee upcoming stress-producing job situations and events and, if possible, try to schedule them so they all do not occur at the same time.

They realistically expect that there will inevitably be some unanticipated stress situations and try to leave some coping time and capacity open for them.

Many of the competent copers compartmentalize work life and home life. They work hard on the job but, once home, they take their attention away from any job pressures and problems by becoming involved at home, for example, with reading, gardening, photography, embroidery, or other hobbies.

And most engage in physical exercise as an aid in releasing tension and building health. The building of health also means building coping energy.

## The Hans Selye Concept: Altruistic Egoism*

To time-honored procedures for the mastery of stress we have recently added a code of behavior described as "altruistic egoism." It is independent of, but compatible with, all religions and political doctrines, being based exclusively on biological laws regulating stress resistance on the cellular level.

In essence, it accepts that all living creatures are, and must be, primarily selfish: the big fish have to eat little fish or they will perish.

None of us can expect others to look after us more than after themselves. However, we must meticulously avoid reckless selfishness, the kind that would induce a hooligan to kill a poor old widow for a few dollars in her piggy bank as long as he is sure that nobody can catch him. I object to this type of egoism not merely on moral grounds, for moralizing is not the domain of the physician, but also because reckless egoism is biologically unsound; it creates so many enemies and such feelings of uncertainty that it could never be a satisfactory permanent guide through life.

* Hans Selye, M.D., Ph.D., SC:, excerpts from a special article in *Medical Times*, 104:11, based on lectures given at Harvard University.

However, we can rid ourselves of guilt feelings and inferiority complexes caused by our inability to be ideal altruists, once we admit that egoism is an inescapable feature of all living beings. It is indispensable for the maintenance of both the individual and the species.

We must have a definite aim in life which we consider worth pursuing, in order to give vent to our innate desire for accomplishment, self-expression, and creativity in whatever occupation we choose.

It is biologically impossible to accept the command "Love thy neighbor as thyself" literally. Man can die on command on the battlefield (as did the kamikaze pilots in the service of their emperor); he can die on command as a martyr in the service of whatever god he accepts, but he cannot love on command. It is up to our neighbors to make themselves lovable.

This code of behavior, based on altruistic egoism, tries to satisfy the natural egoistic tendencies of hoarding capital for security. Most animals hoard food or building materials to assure their homeostasis at future times of need. However, in the case of man, this capital need not necessarily be stocked in the form of dollars, social position, or powerful weaponry—all of which may be taken from us or become obsolete—but in the form of love and goodwill, by learning to become useful to others.

I believe that this can be done while still preserving the time-honored wisdom of the golden rule by translating it into a scientifically acceptable language. The ancient Hebrew version of "Love thy neighbor as thyself" may be translated, without loss of content, into modern language, understandable to all contemporary people.

Similarly, the essence of this unassailable law of behavior can be retained and even enlarged into a motivating guideline if we merely phrase it in terms of the scientifically oriented thinking of our time.

We need only to slightly rephrase it to: "*Earn* thy neighbor's love."

This will best assure homeostasis and resistance to stressors throughout life and give a satisfactory purpose to our activities. It will remove the need of finding destructive outlets or refuge from distasteful activities by resorting to violence, alcohol, or psychedelic drugs, which are at the root of "the crisis of our time."

We have to recognize that man must work, man must be selfish and hoard capital to assure his security.

But who will blame him whose egoistic and capitalistic tendencies express themselves in the insatiable desire to accumulate the goodwill, esteem, and love of others, by helping them, even if he is motivated by altruistic egoism?

## Cognitive Therapy

About 10 years ago an approach to psychotherapy, called cognitive therapy, was developed by Dr. Aaron T. Beck. Based on the theory that negative thought patterns, activated by stress, are integral to a depressive state, this therapy has been producing very promising results.

The idea of cognitive therapy is to pinpoint a depressed patient's specific sensitivities, overreactions, and faulty premises and teach her or him to correct the cognitive distortions. In this way, negative thoughts, such as "I'm wicked and unworthy of anything good," "The world is a terrible place," or "Things can't get any better," can be put aside before they lead to serious depression.

In the research that led to cognitive therapy, Dr. Beck and his colleagues interviewed many depressed patients and found that they often described themselves as losers, lacking essential attributes for reaching life goals, even when in reality this was not true.

Beck found that these people's conclusions were gross distortions. He and his colleagues also found that when depressed people had a number of successful experiences—even the successful performance of a simple card-sorting task—they began to look upon themselves more positively and rated themselves as more competent, attractive, sociable, and optimistic than before the experiment. He describes the therapy:

> By using a combination of verbal and behavioral techniques, we have found that as a person learns to think more realistically, to approach his problems with more perspective, and to look at his future more objectively, his mood improves, while other symptoms such as loss of appetite and insomnia diminish. We call our treatment cognitive therapy because it is aimed at correcting a person's distorted ideas, interpretations and attitudes—in other words, his cognitions.

In cognitive therapy, the patients keep diaries. By writing down their thoughts whenever they feel especially sad or despairing, they learn to identify their self-criticisms and to challenge them.

They may also keep a mastery and pleasure log, a notebook in which they write down their activities as they occur and indicate whether or not they constitute real accomplishments and reasons for satisfaction. Commonly, they find they are accomplishing much more and having more pleasant experiences than they had realized; that they had selective recall for failure or unpleasantness rather than for success and pleasantness; that their low moods had been related to negative thoughts and that by changing their thinking, they can improve their mood.

In Dr. Beck's words: Cognitive therapy works first to uncover a person's negative distortions; then to show him the fallacy in his thinking; next to help him substitute appropriate interpretations for his faulty thinking; and finally to identify and correct the basic unreasonable assumptions that caused his distorted appraisal of reality.

## Changing the Language and Thinking of Stress

Competent copers have their attributes.

Those who do not cope well, who suffer from stress, also have theirs. Among these, certain patterns of thinking and perceiving, which need not be immutable, are emphasized by Dr. Frank Gardner, a Hofstra University Health Center psychologist specializing in stress.*

Emotional stress immediately follows, not a situation, but rather, what an individual tells him- or herself about that situation. Gardner notes, "I've never seen anyone in a coma feel tense. We have to think to feel."

And, because it is a medium of thought, language is important in stress reactions. "There is a great deal of evidence that the words we use to describe things affect our emotional responses," Gardner explains. "We respond to the

* Frank Gardner, *The Hofstra Report*, vol. 7, no. 1, February 1981.

messages we tell ourselves. We appraise things via language."

Often, stressed people repeat to themselves such messages as "This is terrible (or dreadful, or unbearable). Life shouldn't put things in my way which are terrible to me. Why do 'they' keep messing up my life!" These are stress-producing and stress-accentuating messages.

To cope with such thoughts, it is essential to be aware of them. "You have to separate the situation and your reaction to the situation," says Gardner. "We make a lot of assumptions—and a lot of illogical inferences from those assumptions."

Typically, Gardner finds, either one of two treacherous thinking and perceiving patterns, black-and-white thinking and catastrophizing, can contribute significantly to stress.

People who see the world in black-and-white absolutes, of good and bad, of should's and shouldn'ts, pave their way to angry feelings. "On an intellectual level we all know that the world can't always be the way we want, but in a situation we don't always act that way," Gardner says. "The world is *supposed* to be 'screwed up'! Take this sentence with you; it will make you much happier."

Black-and-white thinking sometimes turns back on the self in frustrated perfectionism. But it's important to accept human fallibility. "The best accountant is going to add wrong sometimes; the best therapist is going to misdiagnose sometimes. There's nothing wrong in desiring, only in *demanding*, to be the best."

Catastrophizing blows up things out of proportion and leads to anxiety, or, as Gardner puts it, "expectations of horror." People with such tendencies see a scratch on their car and fear that the entire chassis is about to fall apart.

"You have a right to be tense and angry. Sometimes you may want to go with the feelings. I am not saying things don't matter," Gardner points out, "but that there's a more appropriate 'in-between' reaction. Instead of being highly

## We have to think to feel.

# You have to separate the situation and your reaction to the situation.

anxious, be somewhat aroused; instead of being furious, be somewhat annoyed."

Try new ways, he urges, and expect you may have to argue with yourself as you try. "At first when you say to yourself, 'It isn't that bad,' there may be a little voice telling you, 'It really *is* terrible!'"

Try new ways first on the little things. "The little things are really what take the toll, the nudgy little things that happen all the time," says Gardner.

Have a go at annoyances first for a reason even more significant than their abundance. "People get into a rut. They don't believe they can do something." Early successes with a little annoyance can demonstrate that doing something isn't impossible and can encourage continued change.

# COPING AIDS

**F**or many years at Executive Health Examiners we have seen among our executive clients a man who, at 48, has had a long history of stress-induced problems.

Three years ago, he purchased a jumping jogger, a device somewhat like a minitrampoline which is designed, not to propel into the air, but rather, to absorb shock.

He started out jumping on it 10 minutes a day. Gradually, he increased the time to half an hour daily. And he has adhered, 7 days a week, to a regimen of putting on a tape of his liking at the moment—jazz, pop, disco—and jumping, jogging, swinging his legs, doing a variety of active maneuvers on the jogger, the variety designed to keep him from getting bored with some one activity.

The results have been quite remarkable. He no longer is plagued by his old stress-induced, chronic, low back pains and his gastrointestinal upsets. And he reports enthusiastically that such stress and anxiety reactions as intermittent sweating and tremulousness have also disappeared completely. Not least of all, too, we have noticed a continuing improvement, year after year, in his performance on the treadmill heart-stress test.

We are seeing more and more executives like him—men, and now women as well, who, on their own or as a result of suggestions by our medical staff, have taken up some regular physical activity as a significant means of letting off steam, lowering their arousal levels, and avoiding distress from the stress they face.

## Exercise as Antidote

Many studies have established that physical activity is one of the best antidotes for mental and emotional tension; that it

**183**

# Physical exercise is one of the best antidotes to mental and emotional tension.

is difficult, if not impossible, to remain tense during vigorous activity.

At the University of Southern California some years ago, Dr. Herbert de Vries set about comparing the effects of exercise with those of tranquilizers. In a tense, emotionally upset person, almost invariably muscles become tense. Measuring muscle tension offers an effective, objective method of determining emotional state and any changes in it. De Vries found that even as little exercise as a 15-minute walk is more relaxing than a tranquilizer.

That was no unexpected discovery. Many years ago, the distinguished heart specialist and physician to presidents, Paul Dudley White, observed:

> It has been said that a 5-mile walk will do more good to an unhappy but otherwise healthy man than all the medicine and psychology in the world. Certainly it is true that, in my own case, nervous stress and strain can be counteracted and even prevented by regular vigorous exercise. It is my strong belief that all healthy persons, male and female, should exercise regularly no matter what their ages.

When, a few years ago, Thaddeus Kostrubala, a psychiatrist at Mercy Medical Center, San Diego, decided that he needed regular exercise, he took up running. Before long, some of his psychiatric patients were running along with him three times a week, an hour at a time. Changes in the patients, he has reported, were striking. Those with depression had fewer symptoms; even a schizophrenic patient could be taken off medication.

In studies at the University of Wisconsin Medical School, investigators reported finding that 30 to 45 minutes of jogging three times a week is at least as effective as talk therapy for the moderately depressed.

At the University of Arizona Medical School, Dr. William P. Morgan has found exercise effective in decreasing anxiety.

One of the stressors many of us suffer from is that of our pent-up aggressive drives. When those drives are expressed in physical action, we're likely to be better off.

One EHE client, the chief executive officer of a major New York City advertising agency, now in his early fifties, keeps very fit by skipping rope during the week and chopping wood every weekend. He is especially fond of the chopping, which he says is a great tension-breaker because of the impact, the striking of the logs.

In fact, some physicians at Executive Health Examiners, noting a marked increase in the popularity of indoor racket sports, such as racquetball, among executives, consider that it may be due not only to the vigorous play but also to the great release of tension one gets from striking something.


## Other Values

Regular exercise can help overcome excessive fatigue.

Physically, it helps by enhancing muscular strength and endurance, of course, and additionally by increasing coordination and efficiency of body movement.

Fatigue, moreover, often has psychological aspects. The human body has the capacity to generate as much as 14 horsepower with maximum effort but generates only $\frac{1}{10}$ horsepower at rest, according to studies by Dr. Peter Karpovich, professor of physiology at Springfield College. In many sedentary people, unused horsepower builds into tension, which then becomes a factor in fatigue as well as other complaints. By counteracting tension, exercise may reduce undue fatigue.

The American Heart Association's Committee on Exercise reports that regular, vigorous activity enhances the quality of life by increasing the capacity for both work and play.

There is evidence, too, that physical activity may improve the quality of sleep.

The American Heart Association's Committee on Exercise reports that regular, vigorous activity enhances the quality of life by increasing the capacity for both work and play.

Working with a group of people accustomed to regular exercise, Dr. Frederick Baekeland of the State University of New York Downstate Medical Center, Brooklyn, monitored their sleep in a sleep laboratory during a period when they were engaging in their customary exercise and again during a month-long period when all exercise was banned.

During that month without exercise, the subjects complained that they did not sleep as well. Monitoring instruments also revealed a basic change in sleep patterns: less deep sleep, indicating anxiety, during the no-exercise period.

Evidence that the more a person exercises, the deeper the sleep has also been shown in studies by Dr. R. B. Zloty of the University of Manitoba, Canada, and Dr. Colin Shapiro of Johannesburg, South Africa.

Certainly, not least of all, there is a growing body of evidence of the value of exercise for the heart, for improving its working efficiency and for helping to reduce the risk of disease which can lead to heart attack.

Among the studies is the government's long-term investigation in Framingham, Massachusetts. It has been following the health of more than 5000 people there for more than 25 years. Framingham findings indicate that the most sedentary persons have a death rate from heart disease 5 times greater than that of the most active people.

## Which Activities?

Almost any form of exercise, if practiced regularly, can serve as an antidote to stress.

There is a growing body of evidence of the value of exercise to the heart.

Possible exceptions may be competitive sports for those who tend to be compulsive about achieving a standard of performance or about winning. For them, it's possible for recreational athletic activities to become as stressful as work pressures.

Aerobic exercise, including running, jogging, brisk walking, swimming, cycling, or any activity that is rhythmic and leads to a sustained increase in breathing and heart rate, is valuable for relieving stress and at the same time may be helpful for the heart.

Mild exercise, too, such as calisthenics performed during exercise breaks a few times a day, can be useful in relieving stress-produced tension.

One important precaution: For anyone over 35 who has long been sedentary, there should be no sudden leap into full-fledged, vigorous activity. Instead, proceed slowly, gradually increasing the intensity—preferably after clearance following a medical checkup.

## Relaxation Therapy

### Breathing, a Simple Aid

Breathing techniques are part of many effective forms of relaxation therapy. They may also be of value in themselves.

A regular, relaxed, slow pattern of breathing—moving the diaphragm rather than the upper chest—helps to lower the arousal level. It can almost immediately change many of the physical indicators of a stress response. For example, skin response to an electric stimulus diminishes while skin temperature rises.

Dr. Leon J. Warshaw, an occupational health physician, recalls that early in his career he encountered people who were building up tension and anxiety to the point of interfering with their performance and producing discomfort. It was, he knew, futile to tell them to "just relax." They had heard that many times. So he devised what he calls "a little ritual."

Asking his patients to close their eyes and to stand if they

RELAXED
BREATHING:
TWO HELPFUL
EXERCISES
TO HALT
TENSION

- Lie on the floor on your back, belt or girdle loose, spine straight, head raised slightly on a pillow, knees bent, feet flat on the floor about 8 inches apart. With one hand on your stomach and the other on your chest, inhale so as to draw a deep breath into your stomach. Your chest should scarcely move; the stomach should rise.

As this procedure becomes easier and easier and you take long slow breaths into your stomach, breathing in through your nose and out through your mouth, add a sound of "Haaaah" as you let your jaw and mouth hang slightly open (without strain).

Practice the first exercise for several minutes at a time.

- For half a dozen or more times, still in the same position on the floor, make a deep sighing sound and allow all the air to empty out of your lungs. Then, without any ef-fort to inhale, let the air come back in.

Once you find breathing into your stomach becoming almost natural, go a step further. Whenever you have an opportunity, several times a day, practice just taking three or four deep, slow, into-the-stomach breaths as you concentrate on relaxation of breathing.

And now, as you find yourself experiencing a relaxed feeling from the deliberate, easy, slow, into-the-stomach breathing, make use of it any time you begin to feel tension building up.

Use it in the office, at home, in the car, or anywhere else, any time you get any kind of hint that you're becoming upset.

Try it, too, if you should feel a tension headache about to come on or an ache starting low in your back.

did most of their work sitting or to sit if they usually stood or walked about while working, he had them breathe in and out slowly and rhythmically, counting silently or aloud as they preferred, until they reached some number, such as

Research findings indicate that sedentary persons have a death rate from heart disease five times greater than active people.

> # Anyone over 35 should take no sudden leap into full-fledged, vigorous activity.

100. In tough cases, he had them start with a higher number and count back to zero. Often, while they breathed in such a pattern, he had them bend and extend their arms, shoulders, and neck slowly and gently.

The breathing exercise, which took only a few minutes, was repeated several times a day. Furthermore, there were strict instructions that during the exercise period, no calls were to be taken or interruptions allowed. Says Dr. Warshaw:

> I have no recollection of where I learned about this remedy; since then, I have encountered more than a few clinicians who prescribed it in one form or another. It seemed like such a simple, commonsense procedure that I never did any research to find out how often and why it worked. The important thing is that whenever it was practiced faithfully, the results were almost uniformly good. Recently, more than two decades after I taught it to them, I met two people who reported that they still benefit from its use.

Some executives find relaxation breathing a valuable adjunct to exercise. Used before and after, they report, the easy, slow, rhythmic, and relaxed breathing seems to increase the benefits of physical activity.

### Progressive Relaxation: Mind and Muscles

For more than half a century, Dr. Edmund Jacobson, a physiologist, has been advocating and teaching progressive relaxation based on his research into mind-muscle relationships. His studies indicate that muscles can have potent effects on such mental activities as attention, awareness, and imagination.

He has developed a major thesis: that relaxation and anxiety are mutually exclusive. They cannot coexist. When muscles are truly relaxed, there can be no anxiety.

Because, generally, we have little, if any, appreciation of the sensation of relaxation, Jacobson's progressive relaxation is based upon tensing and releasing different muscles in the body so the sensation of tension can be contrasted with that of relaxing and letting go.

To use the technique, a subject is asked to start by tensing a set of muscles as hard as possible until the tension and even muscle tenderness and pain can be felt. Then the subject lets those muscles relax and tries to experience internally—feel—the difference between tension and relaxation.

For example, in one exercise, you bend your wrist so that the back of your hand is directed toward the top of your forearm. As much as you can, you tense the muscles forcing the hand backward. And you hold the muscles tense until you may feel tenderness in muscles of the middle and upper forearm. Then you release the tension by letting your hand fall down to a relaxed, loose position.

The same procedure is used with other sets of muscles until the subject learns to tense and relax muscles from head to toe.

### A Simple Technique: Relaxing with a Memory

At the University of California at Davis, Drs. Alfred P. French and J. P. Tupin have developed a simple, meditationlike re-

Studies indicate that muscles can have potent effects on attention, awareness, and imagination.

laxation method that may be learned in a few minutes and that often is helpful in relieving moderate anxiety. Often, report French and Tupin, the technique is also effective in relieving insomnia, moderate pain, and emotional responses to illness.

They suggest this three-step method:

* *First, sit comfortably with feet on the floor and eyes closed, and relax your breathing —really letting your breathing become relaxed so that air flows gently into and out of your lungs, after which you can allow your muscles to relax.*

* *Next, simply allow your mind to be as relaxed as your muscles are, and let your mind drift, very naturally and very gently, in the direction of a memory which is very pleasant, relaxing, restful, and reassuring. In most cases, this becomes possible within a minute.*

* *Finally, simply present that memory very gently to your mind. Allow yourself to be there and experience that memory. Don't concentrate or think about it in the usual sense, and if your mind wanders off simply bring yourself back, very gently and naturally, by presenting the memory to your mind again.*

The method usually is learned in 3 or 4 minutes and, French and Tupin find, in many cases it produces an immediate sense of both relaxation and well-being.

### Meditation: Using It to Unwind

Several years ago, in its business pages, the *New York Times* ran a story headed "Management: Using Meditation to Unwind." The article noted that at 6 o'clock every morning, the board chairman of a major midwestern brewery settles himself into an easy chair, closes his eyes and, for 20 minutes, meditates, silently repeating his mantra (a phrase chanted repeatedly) and keeping his mind free of all but the most fleeting thoughts. Before dinner that evening, he repeats the procedure.

Meditation, he says, tunes up his mind, prevents him from getting "worn out," and helps him keep cool under stress, according to the *Times* report.

Meanwhile, in his Manhattan apartment, a partner in a large accounting firm wakes at 6:30 A.M., moves to a chair near his bed, and meditates for 20 minutes. Later, he spends another 20 minutes meditating in his office.

Although he calls himself a "devout skeptic" by nature, he reported to the *Times:* "Now I react very differently to a stressful situation. Occasionally in my work, there'll be somebody yelling at the other end of a phone, or something will come up that is really high pressure. I have no anxiety in the pit of my stomach. I can handle it more efficiently and more easily."

Also reporting to the *Times*, the manager of branch operations for one of America's largest corporations, says that he meditates at 5:45 A.M. at home, and again at 2:30 in the afternoon, sitting on a couch in his office.

"I don't understand all the physiological things that occur," he says, "but I know I'm a lot sharper and more acute. My retention level is higher. I'm not a faddist, and I didn't go into this for a couple of years after hearing about it, but it's done wonders for me."

The three businessmen are graduates of a formal transcendental meditation class. Clearly, TM is not for everyone. For example, fully half of one group of insurance company executives who began the practice were dropouts within a few months.

But enthusiasts can be passionate about the benefits not only of TM but of other forms of meditation, notably the relaxation response and a technique called CSM (clinically standardized meditation).

## Transcendental Meditation

In 1959, Maharishi Mahesh Yogi, a guru who early in his life had studied physics, left India, bringing with him a revised form of yoga. He set up an organization to train instructors

Meditation enthusiasts can be passionate about the benefits not only of TM, but also of other forms of meditation—notably, the relaxation response and CSM.

who in turn could teach his technique. By the early 1970s, an estimated 10,000 Americans a month were getting training in transcendental meditation (TM).

TM requires no intense concentration, no rigorous mental or physical control, and the relatively simple technique is easily learned.

It has four essential elements: quiet surroundings, a passive attitude, a comfortable sitting position, and a mental device. The device is a secret word, the mantra—a sound or phrase which is given to you by an instructor and which you promise not to divulge. It is often derived from Hindu scripture and allegedly is chosen to suit the individual.

In two 20-minute periods a day, one in the morning, usually before breakfast, and one in the evening, usually before dinner, the meditator, sitting comfortably, repeats the mantra over and over silently as an aid in preventing distracting thoughts. If such thoughts come into mind, the meditator disregards them, going back to the mantra.

Feelings produced by TM can vary considerably. Some people experience feelings of restfulness and quiet, others a sense of pleasure and well-being, and still others report a feeling of nearly ecstatic deep relaxation.

Various physiological effects may occur. Often, oxygen consumption falls off by 10 to 20 percent much as during sleep, reflecting a drop in body metabolism. Heartbeat slows and breathing rate and depth decline. Blood pressure drops, especially when it is high to begin with.

One of the major benefits claimed for TM is that it eases stress. There have been reports, too, of improvement in job performance, significant reduction in high blood pressure, peptic ulcer healing, curing of insomnia, and relief of many stress-related disorders.

Some critics wonder whether comparable results might not be achieved simply by two daily periods of rest. In one study by Dr. R. R. Michaels and other University of Michigan investigators, attention centered on blood values for the hormones epinephrine and norepinephrine, which are released in association with stress and lend themselves to measurement.

Measurements were made before, during, and after meditation in twelve subjects—six men and six women—all formally trained in TM. Nine were qualified as TM teachers by the originator of the technique, Maharishi Mahesh Yogi. Values for the hormones were compared with those obtained from control subjects matched for sex and age who rested instead of meditating. The investigators reported: Essentially the same results were obtained for the two groups, which suggests that meditation does not induce a unique metabolic state, but is seen biochemically as a resting state.

Nevertheless, as many critics remark, there is no denying the usefulness of TM. As one has put it: "Practicing transcendental meditation twice daily is the first time Americans have ever sat still and focused on their minds, and one easily could expect to see physiologic changes resulting from this voluntary regimen of inactivity."

## The Relaxation Response

Herbert Benson, M.D., director of the Hypertension and Behavioral Medicine Sections at Boston's Beth Israel Hospital, studied TM and confirmed its value in reducing tension and high blood pressure. But he became convinced that meditation could be as useful as TM when stripped of the latter's mysticism. It could be used, quite simply, in noncultic fashion, to elicit what he calls an innate *relaxation response*.

There is, of course, the innate *fight-or-flight* response, a physiological reaction to danger which raises blood pressure, heart rate, and breathing, speeds blood flow to muscles, and prepares the body to fight or run. Useful to early humans against physical threats in the environment, it is less necessary in the modern world where stresses are largely mental. Yet, it's the triggering of that response by mental and emotional stressors that may cause hypertension and stress disorders in some people.

On the other hand, Benson believes, there is also an innate relaxation response that has the opposite physical effect to fight-or-flight; it slows the heart and breathing rates and reduces the tension in the circulatory system. Relatively simple meditation can induce this response.

The Benson procedure shares with TM the four essential elements of quiet surroundings, passive attitude, comfortable sitting position, and mental device, which in this case is just the word "one."

Benson teaches patients to sit quietly in a comfortable position with eyes closed, to deeply relax all muscles, beginning at the feet and progressing up to the face, and to keep them relaxed.

The patients are then instructed to breathe through the nose, to become aware of the breathing, and, as they breathe out, to say the word, "one" silently to themselves. They are to continue doing this for 10 to 20 minutes.

Benson further instructs:

* *You may open your eyes to check the time, but do not use an alarm. When you finish, sit quietly for several minutes, at first with your eyes closed and later with your eyes opened. Do not stand up for a few minutes.*

* *Do not worry about whether you are successful in achieving a deep level of relaxation. Maintain a passive attitude and permit relaxation to occur at its own pace. When distracting thoughts occur, try to ignore them by not dwelling upon them and return to repeating "one." With practice, the response should come with little effort. Practice the technique once or twice daily, but not within 2 hours after any meal, since the digestive processes seem to interfere with the elicitation of the relaxation response.*

What feelings accompany the relaxation response? They vary, Benson reports. Most people feel a sense of calm and great relaxation. A small percentage experience ecstatic feelings. Various individuals have told of feelings of pleasure, refreshment, and well-being. Still others have noted relatively little change in feelings. But, regardless of reported feelings, Benson notes, the physiological changes, such as decreased oxygen consumption, take place. He maintains:

> The case for the use of the relaxation response by healthy but harassed individuals is straightforward. It can act as a built-in method of counteracting the stresses of everyday living which bring forth the fight-or-flight response. We have also shown how the relaxation response may be used as a new approach to aid in the treatment and perhaps prevention of diseases such as hypertension.

## A Test of the Relaxation Response

A 12-week investigation of the relaxation response took place in the corporate offices of a company in Wilmington, Massachusetts. It was carried out by Dr. Ruanne Peters, a Harvard research fellow, in collaboration with Dr. Benson.

The participants were 140 employees who volunteered and another 54 "nonvolunteers" selected randomly and asked to take part in a very limited way. The volunteers and nonvolunteers, 54 percent female and 46 percent male, averaged 33 years of age, and 63 percent were married. Of the group, 23 percent held managerial or supervisory positions; 29 percent were technical specialists; and 48 percent held clerical positions.

The volunteers kept daily records and attended biweekly sessions at which their blood pressures were measured, and they filled out self-assessment questionnaires on their general health, work performance, and well-being. Nonvolunteers had their blood pressures measured only at the beginning and the end of the study.

The volunteers were separated on a random basis into groups A, B, and C. The nonvolunteers became group D. Only group A was taught the technique of eliciting the relaxation response. Group B was instructed to sit quietly and relax. Groups C and D received no instructions and were told to follow their usual schedule.

Over the test period, groups A and B took two 15-minute breaks a day, one in the morning and one in the afternoon or evening, either at work or at home. Group A was asked to practice the relaxation response technique; group B to relax without using any particular technique; and groups C and D took no relaxation breaks.

When the data were analyzed, it turned out that significant decreases in blood pressure occurred only in group A. Group B experienced lowered pressure but to a lesser extent. In groups C and D, there was very little or no change. This pattern of blood pressure changes among the groups appeared in both sexes, at all ages, and from all levels of initial pressure, but, especially in group A, greater decreases tended to occur in those who had higher blood pressure to begin with.

The same pattern of changes was noted on the indexes of general health, overall performance, and sense of well-being. The greatest average improvements on each of these occurred in group A, followed by groups B and C respectively.

### Clinically Standardized Meditation

Clinically standardized meditation (CSM) is a variation of transcendental meditation developed by Dr. Patricia Carrington, Princeton University lecturer in psychology. It falls somewhere between TM and the Benson relaxation response.

Like Benson, Dr. Carrington brushes aside TM's mysticism and secretiveness. But, she believes that meditation, like TM, can be learned more effectively and quickly when taught by a qualified, experienced "supervisor." She encourages patients to use the self-instructional audiocassettes that she has developed for home reinforcement of the CSM technique.

With CSM, a subject may choose a mantra from a list or devise one. Dr. Carrington's nonsecret mantras are usually melodic words or nonsense syllables (such as "vis-ta," "shan-ti," "shi-rim") rated by volunteers as pleasant and soothing.

CSM is permissive. No effort need be made to concentrate on the mantra or coordinate its use with breathing. And distracting thoughts are allowed to drift in and out of consciousness while the subject attends passively to the sound of the mantra. This permissiveness, Dr. Carrington believes, allows subjects to desensitize themselves to disturbing thoughts.

One indication of the efficacy of CSM is a program to treat a group of New York Telephone Company employees who reported very high levels of on-the-job stress. With CSM training, they experienced a marked decrease in anxiety, in hostility and depression, and in physical symptoms associated with stress. The firm has adopted CSM training in a companywide stress-reduction program.

## Biofeedback

Biofeedback is, in effect, an extension of the normal way in which we learn.

In learning, we receive "feedback" cues from such sources as our eyes, ears, hands, and feet. Swing a golf club, for example, and you feel your arms move, see how the club connects with the ball, and watch where the ball goes—all cues to guide you so you can try to correct your swing for possibly better ball placement next time.

In most people, the face tends to be extraordinarily expressive of mood and emotion. Some people have argued quite seriously that the body feels what the face feels; that the face may be the key cue to the rest of the body.

# Biofeedback is an extension of the normal way we live.

Usually, however, we get few feedback cues to what goes on within the body. But sensitive electronic equipment can provide such awareness. With electrodes attached at various points on the body, the equipment can detect, amplify, and display small internal fluctuations in the form of sound beeps or light flashes, for example.

The potential of biofeedback is very closely tied to what has amounted to a virtual revolution in an old medical theory. That theory held that the human being is unable consciously to exert control over the autonomic nervous system. Ordinarily, without our awareness, this system regulates such processes as pulse rate, the secretions of glands, oxygen consumption, and other complex mechanisms which, upon being disturbed, often trigger stress disorders.

This theory was challenged, however, by Dr. Neal E. Miller of Rockefeller University. By drugging rats with curare to inactivate their skeletal muscles, then using electric shock as a teaching aid, Miller and his coworkers established that the rats could be taught to control interior processes.

Rats, it turned out, can learn to control blood pressure levels to obtain suitable awards. Miller even had one rat which could be regularly brought to send enough blood to one ear to produce a blush there, while the other ear blanched.

At the Menninger Foundation in Topeka, Kansas, one of the first institutions to study the use of biofeedback for migraine headaches, notable successes have been achieved by taping temperature sensors to a patient's finger and forehead. A meter shows the difference between head and hand temperature.

While watching the meter, the patient is asked to do such things as relax while repeating a calming phrase (such as "I feel quiet") in order to relax blood vessels in the hands and thus increase hand temperature. When he or she succeeds, the meter needle moves. With the relaxation and warming of the hands comes a redistribution of blood that reduces pressure in blood vessels in the head, ending the migraine headache.

Once a patient develops the ability to move the needle, the same technique can be used, without the biofeedback equipment, to cut short a migraine episode.

Investigators at Menninger have reported that 74 percent of migraine sufferers have improved and have gained the ability to increase blood in the hands in almost 100 percent of situations in which they detect the onset of a headache.

Biofeedback has also been found to work well for tension headaches, which are the most common kind, involving contraction of forehead, scalp, and neck muscles. Improvement rates of up to 80 percent have been reported.

Patients with tension headaches may have sensor electrodes applied to the forehead to record muscle tension. If the level is high, the biofeedback equipment emits a series of rapid beeps that the patients hear through earphones. As tension is reduced, the beeps slow.

Biofeedback gives a patient a precise measurement of his or her physical state as it pertains to headaches. It also offers the gratification of knowing that the sufferer can alter that state. In effect, the signal beeping at the desired pace tells a patient, "You're in charge of yourself."

Biofeedback is still an art rather than a science. Much research remains to be done. Still, biofeedback currently is in wide use for treating stress-related disorders such as migraine and tension headaches and in rehabilitation of persons with nerve-and-muscle disorders such as the paralysis that accompanies stroke. It is being used and studied for a number of other problems, too.

Muscle biofeedback is one of the forms of biofeedback which seems most promising to many investigators. It is concerned mainly with learning to decrease muscle tension, as in relaxation, or to increase muscle activity to regain muscle function, as in rehabilitation from partial paralysis.

Biofeedback of muscle activity is usually called EMG biofeedback (from the acronym for electromyogram, which is a recorded pattern of muscle electrical activity). For EMG biofeedback, sensors are placed on the skin over an appropriate muscle and the electrical signals from the underlying muscles are fed to the biofeedback instrument to be amplified and to activate an auditory or visual signal.

Among the disorders other than tension headaches for which EMG biofeedback shows promise, according to reports from various investigators, are anxiety, phobias, insomnia, alcoholism, drug abuse, asthma, high blood pressure, menstrual distress, and some intestinal disorders such as ulcer or colitis.

An example of the interesting research work going on is a study by Dr. Herbert Krauss, consultant to Executive Health Examiners. Krauss administered a test to a group of subjects designed to measure their trait, or chronic, level of anxiety. He then attached biofeedback sensors to the frontalis muscles in the subjects' foreheads and had them work with the biofeedback equipment to relax those muscles. The result: a very much lower anxiety and tension level.

## Modifying Type A Behavior

Type A behavior, as we have seen earlier, is now recognized as a major risk factor for coronary heart disease and heart attack. Additionally, it can be an internal source of pressure and stress. It is a behavior common to many executives.

Can it be modified?

Research is now under way on a substantial scale to evaluate methods for modification and the benefits of modification as well. At Colorado State University and the University of Montreal, studies with coronary heart disease patients have shown significant reductions in blood pressure and blood cholesterol levels following Type A modification. In a study at the U.S. Naval Hospital in San Diego, a modification program was set up as part of post–heart attack rehabilitation. Participants showed significantly less heart morbidity and mortality than post–heart attack patients who received only standard rehabilitation measures.

In what is believed to be the first mass attempt to alter the A behavior pattern, Dr. Meyer Friedman, one of the pioneers in the study of Type A behavior, is working with 900 post–heart attack patients. Both Friedman and Ray H. Rosenman, M.D., another pioneer investigator of Type A, believe modification is possible but not easy.

One difficulty is that the Type A person tends to have what Friedman calls "some vague sort of Horatio Alger complex." Such a person believes that the complex—the competitive drive, time urgency, speed, and hyperarousal—has been primarily responsible for his or her major accomplishments and that any change will lead to diminished income, power, and prestige.

When Type A people finally recognize the true nature of their behavior, they try to modify it. "They begin to realize that Type A behavior has actually impeded their socioeconomic progress rather than enhanced it," Dr. Friedman observes. "They become aware that this behavior may be a failure-inducing, not a success-producing, pattern."

It is also helpful when the patient realizes that Type A behavior over many years may have impoverished various aspects of personality. Friedman points to Charles Darwin who, when he discovered that sad fact about himself, wrote:

> My mind seems to have become a machine for grinding out large collections of facts, but why this should have caused the atrophy of that part of the brain alone on which higher tastes depend, I cannot conceive. . . . The loss of these tastes (the enjoyment of poetry, music, painting, reading of general literature, etc.) is a loss of happiness and may be enfeebling the emotional part of my nature.

Two other realizations can be critical. One is that modification does not mean changing a Type A person into a Type B but, rather, tempering the A behavior. The second is that, with modification, there can be not only a reduction in coronary heart disease risk and self-induced stress but also gains in efficiency and productivity, along with gains in general health, sense of well-being, and life satisfactions.

Evidence that this is so comes from the Montreal study, mentioned earlier, in which participants went on working the same number of hours and carrying the same responsibilities as before behavior modification but reported enjoying life more now.

## Modification Strategies

Techniques for helping Type A executives to evaluate and make useful changes in their behavior are being developed and tested. It will be years before the long-term results can be determined, but short-term results are often excellent and there is reason to expect them to persist.

Changing Type A behavior may best be done with the aid of a trained counselor. But, short of that, executives who already recognize themselves as Type A or who wish to evaluate themselves and make valuable changes may find the following guidelines useful. They are based upon methods used by Drs. Friedman, Rosenman, and others in a growing number of programs.

*Observing yourself* Often, Type A people are unaware of their actual behavior. Self-observation can be a vital first step.

It can teach you, as Dr. Rosenman puts it, "to witness such daily experiences as the struggle in commuting to work, the schedule bulging with activities without adequate breaks, the battle with the clock, and the impatience and irritation with others that too often are manifested in facial tension and vocal outbursts."

Log yourself. Keep a record, for a week or two, of the situations that make you angry, anxious, or frustrated, or that make you very much aware of the clock and give you a dominating sense of time urgency.

That record can serve several purposes, beginning with helping to motivate you to make changes. It can also pinpoint particular behaviors that most need change and then serve as a kind of benchmark against which you can measure progress.

**Contracting**  One at a time, make a series of small contracts with yourself, written commitments to changing particularly undesirable daily patterns of behavior. There should be no effort to change yourself completely overnight. That is almost certainly doomed to failure.

Instead, take one specific thing at a time. For example: Rather than say in general terms that you are going to slow down at work, determine instead to walk, instead of rush, to work and to walk in a relaxed fashion.

Contract to slow down in other ways—one at a time. For example, practice eating with slower movements, even occasionally putting your fork down between bites. Slow your speech when you talk. Drive more slowly.

Contract to listen to music as an aid in relaxing when you drive rather than to dictate or become frustrated by other drivers. Or, if music programs on the radio, because of talk or commercials, annoy you, choose tape cassettes to your liking.

For at least one coffee break a day, contract to replace the coffee with a brisk walk.

Once or twice a day take time to spend several minutes in muscle relaxation. Tense, then relax the muscles of your hands, arms, face, shoulders, chest, stomach, legs, and focus on the relaxed feeling that comes when muscle tension is released.

Contract, in due course, to get 20 to 30 minutes of exercise a week.

**Evaluating Yourself**  Try to make your self-evaluation a real, perceptive, nonassumptive one. How much of a factor in your success has Type A behavior—your hurry-hurry—actually been? When you really analyze what has gone on, isn't it a fact that your progress has stemmed from other qualities you have? And is it conceivable, seriously, that, if anything, hurry-hurry has been more impediment than asset?

Consider your life's goals. Perhaps determine what they were when you started out and what they really are or might be today if you attend to them seriously now. "Concentrate

on what is worth *being* rather than what is worth *having*,"
somebody has remarked. It might be that you would really
like to follow this suggestion.

***Managing your environment*** Type A people often fail
to manage their environment effectively in terms not only of
getting work done properly but of doing so without causing
themselves distress.

Delegate whenever possible. If that's difficult for you, if
you feel too often that only you can do the task, give delega-
tion a trial anyhow. You may be surprised, and all the more
so if, in delegating, you explain with patience exactly what
must be done.

Eliminate needlessly excessive obligations. Must you
take on so many extra duties, get involved in so many committees at and away from work? Get rid of the trivial.

Try setting priorities the first thing you do each day.
Then stay with them, going from one thing to another in due
course, taking up a new task only when you finish with one
that has higher priority.

Learn how to schedule your appointments realistically,
so you are not always rushing from one to another.

Learn, too, how to manage requests, and even demands,
from others. Let them know how much time and effort you
can give, and when you cannot oblige. One expert in stress
management suggests: "Get the person who wants you to
take on another task to help you evaluate the urgency of the
request and determine where it fits among your priority
items."

Try getting up 15 minutes earlier in the morning so you
can begin the day in less rushed, more relaxed fashion.

When you are up against a deadline, concentrate on the
job. But try taking an occasional break: walk about, chat with
someone, stare quietly out the window for a minute or so—
anything to cut down on the tension. You may well find this
no loss of time at all but an actual time-saver and aid to effective concentration.

***Working at the hostility problem*** "A critical and difficult problem," Dr. Rosenman calls it, "the hostility that often
grows out of excessive impatience and competitiveness. In

the course of development of the Type A behavior pattern, hostile aggressiveness is fostered." He continues:

"Perhaps, because Type A individuals place winning and achievement as the ultimate goals, they perceive most other individuals as competitors and threats. The Type A person's band of hostility may be described as 'free floating,' reflecting its capacity to be touched off by even the slightest provocation."

Rosenman urges Type A people to observe and monitor their frustration, anger, and hostility, noting the situations that provoke them and recording them so they become clear. After doing so, efforts can be made to deal with them.

Are there particular people who especially annoy you? Perhaps, at least some of these people can be avoided. Are you wasting hostility and anger on trivial matters, even those about which you can do little or nothing, such as a delayed plane, a discourteous salesperson, or an inept waiter?

Stop demanding, if only in your mind, that others act as you do, talk as you do, move as you do. Don't interrupt them almost invariably, or finish their sentences for them, again almost invariably.

***Modeling*** An effective way to develop new behavior is to observe a model, to see how some other successful person carries out the behavior, how he or she gets things done in relaxed fashion, exhibiting humor rather than anger, using relaxed rather than frenetic movements.

Perhaps you can select such a model from among your acquaintances. He or she need not be aware of the selection. You can study your model's reactions to daily stressors and his or her handling of them. Imitation can be helpful.

# Drug Treatment

Do drugs have any role in our dealings with our anxiety and feelings of stress?

Anti-anxiety drugs—tranquilizers—sometimes have a place, but they are not, as so many people seem to think, inevitably the answer.

Each year, American pharmacists fill over 150 million prescriptions for mood-affecting drugs. Are they justified?

Perhaps one concerned medical authority is right. He asks these questions:

> How do physicians acquire such unquestioning faith in drugs? Are they stampeded by their patients? Because they serve a public that has been brainwashed to think that there is a "pill for every ill," do they believe the patient will be disappointed if he doesn't receive something tangible in return for sharing his problems?

But he answers these questions thus:

> Many physicians feel ill-equipped to deal with the emotional aspects of a patient's illness and are unwilling to embroil themselves in a lengthy and financially unrewarding discussion with him. No doubt a pill is the easy way out.

> But it is *not* the effective way out.

Tranquilizers, of course, do not cure anxiety. They do not get at the bases for stress disorders. They can relieve symptoms and they may be valuable for that purpose when stress reactions and anxiety become so intense as to interfere with job and other aspects of living.

In some cases, physicians have found tranquilizers valuable when the patient's symptoms, emotional and physical, are so disabling that coherent communication and counseling are virtually impossible.

In other cases, the drugs may be valuable when physical symptoms are so debilitating that a patient is unable to accept the possibility that the manifestations, so suggestive of actual organic disease, may be caused only by the stresses of his or her life. Then, a suitable tranquilizer in appropriate dosage may help, through its relief of the symptoms, to convince the patient of the stress origin and lower the anxiety level enough to facilitate other therapeutic steps.

## Psychotherapy

Psychotherapy certainly is not always needed to combat stress. But it often can be a valuable aid, as noted earlier, for the executive with stress-induced depression. It can be use-

# Psychotherapy can be a valuable aid for the executive with stress-produced depression.

ful, similarly, for stress-provoked anxiety. It need not take the form of extended classic Freudian psychoanalysis, with years spent on the couch. The range of professional help for emotional problems is much broader now.

In actual fact, short-term psychotherapy, consisting of 10 to 15 counseling sessions and sometimes even fewer, often helps during a particularly difficult stress or an emotional situation. It is not uncommon for psychotherapy to bring some, almost immediate, reduction of discomfort. Expressing painful thoughts and feelings to a qualified counselor helps to relieve distress through sharing.

If you should need professional help, your personal physician may be in a position to suggest a suitable therapist.

How do you know if there is such a need?

As a distinguished psychiatrist has put it, summing up well the view of many specialists:

> The key element of when to look for help is to listen to your own inner stirrings. When the intensity of the problem becomes too great to handle yourself or by talking with spouse or trusted friend, then look for professional help.

## Envoi

It's a very fundamental concept.

However much the stress of executive work is—and there is no gainsaying that it is plentiful—it is not, in the final analysis, the stress itself which causes problems. It is how one *reacts* to the stress.

The fundamental concept is, you don't have to respond with distress; you can teach yourself not to. You can, indeed, learn to cope.

# ACKNOWLEDGMENTS

Pages 6–7, A. Mitchell, Stanford Research Institute No. 77–206, National Science Foundation Commissioned Study, 1977. Reprinted by permission of The Stanford Research Institute.

Page 8, Dr. Leonard Cammer, *Uptight: How to Liberate Yourself from Compulsive Behavior*. Published by Simon & Schuster, Inc. Copyright © 1976 by Harold I. Cammer and Robert Cammer, trustees F.B.O. Beatrice Cammer. Reprinted by permission of Simon & Schuster, Inc.

Page 11, by permission of John C. Connelly, M.D.

Pages 12–13, Dr. Elliot Jacques, *Project Health: The Pressure Principle*. Copyright © 1972 by G. D. Searle & Company. Reprinted by permission of G. D. Searle & Company.

Pages 13–14, Dr. Jeremiah A. Barondess, from a seminar on "The Consequences of Stress." Reprinted by permission of Dr. Jeremiah A. Barondess.

Page 14, Kathy Slobogin, "The Human Cost of Stress," *The New York Times Magazine*, November 20, 1977. Copyright © 1977 by The New York Times Company. Reprinted by permission.

Pages 16–17, Dr. Gary E. Schwartz, "Undelivered Warnings." Reprinted from *Psychology Today*, March 1980. Copyright © by Ziff-Davis Publishing Company. Reprinted by permission of Ziff-Davis Publishing Company.

Page 20, Ari Kiev, M.D. and Vera Kohn, *Executive Stress: An AMA Survey Report*, for AMACOM, a division of American Management Associations, 1979. Reprinted by permission of AMACOM.

Pages 21–22, Dr. Steven H. Appelbaum, "Coping with Mental 'Wear and Tear,'" *Occupational Health and Safety*, October 1980. Reprinted by permission of Dr. Steven H. Appelbaum.

Pages 25–27, Dr. John H. Howard, "Stress and the Manager," *Stress*, Vol. 1, No.1. Reprinted by permission of *Stress* and Dr. John H. Howard.

Pages 27–34, by permission of Dr. Herbert Krauss.

Pages 35–36, reprinted by permission of Theodore Lidz, M.D.

Pages 36–37, Stanley H. Cath, M.D., "Suicide in the Middle Years: Some Reflections on the Annihilation of Self," from *Mid Life: Developmental and Clinical Issues*, eds. W. H. Norman and T. J. Scaramella. Published by Brunner/Mael, Inc. Reprinted by permission of W. H. Norman and Brunner/Mael, Inc.

Pages 39–40, Daniel X. Freedman, M.D., from a seminar on "The Consequences of Stress: The Medical and Social Implications of Prescribing Tranquilizers," Cornell University Medical College, 1978. Reprinted by permission of Daniel X. Freedman, M.D.

Pages 45–49, Hans Selye, M.D., "A Syndrome Produced by Diverse Nocuous Agents," *Nature*, 1936. Reprinted by permission of *Nature* and Hans Selye, M.D.

Page 53, Thomas H. Holmes and Richard H. Rahe, "Social Readjustment Rating Scale," *Journal of Psychosomatic Research*, Vol. 11. Copyright 1967 by Pergamon Press, Ltd. Reprinted by permission of Pergamon Press, Ltd.

Page 60, Irving S. Wright, M.D., "Cardiovascular Diseases: Role of Psychogenic and Behavior Patterns in Development and Aggravation," *New York State Journal of Medicine*, October 1975. Reprinted by permission of Irving S. Wright, M.D.

Page 61, James E. Skinner, M.D., "Heart Attack Trigger." Reprinted from *Psychology Today*, July 1980. Copyright © 1980 by Ziff-Davis Publishing Company. Reprinted by permission of Ziff-Davis Publishing Company.

Pages 62–63, Philip Goldberg, "Self-Evaluation: The Glazer-Stress Control Life-Style Questionnaire." Reprinted from *Executive Health*. Copyright © 1978, by McGraw-Hill, Inc., New York, N.Y. 10020. All rights reserved.

Page 66, Meyer Friedman, M.D., "Type A Behavior: A Progress Report," *The Sciences*, February 1980.

Pages 71–72, Dr. David C. Glass, "Stress, Competition, and Heart Attacks." Reprinted from *Psychology Today*, December 1976. Copyright © by Ziff-Davis Publishing Company.

Page 81, Lawrence Galton, *The Silent Disease: Hypertension*. Copyright © 1973 by Crown Publishers, Inc. Reprinted by permission.

Pages 96–97, Dr. William T. Gibb, "Executive Health," Vol. VI, No. 12, 1970. Reprinted by permission of Executive Publications.

Page 98, Walter C. Alvarez, M.D. Reprinted by permission of Luis W. Alvarez.

Page 123, from a seminar on "The Consequences of Stress," New York City, January 1979. Reprinted by permission of Dr. Leo M. Hollister.

Page 127, from a seminar on "The Consequences of Stress," New York City, January 1979. Reprinted by permission of Robert E. Rakel, M.D.

Page 151, Phyllis Moen. Report from New York State College of Human Ecology, Cornell University, May 1981. Reprinted by permission of Phyllis Moen.

Page 153, by permission of Dr. Tobias Brocher.

Pages 155–156, 158, Liz Roman Gallese, "Manager's Journal," *Wall Street Journal*, May 4, 1981. Reprinted by permission of *The Wall Street Journal*. Copyright © Dow Jones & Company, Inc. (1981). All Rights Reserved.

Pages 156–157, Stephen P. Hersh, M.D., *The Executive Parent*. Copyright © 1979 by Stephen P. Hersh, M.D. Reprinted by permission of Sovereign Books, a Simon & Schuster division of Gulf & Western Corporation.

Pages 162–164, Dr. Suzanne Hayes and Dr. Manning Feinleib, *American Journal of Public Health*, Vol. 70, No. 2, February 1980. Reprinted by permission of Dr. Suzanne Hayes, Dr. Manning Feinleib, and the American Public Health Association.

Pages 164–166, Marcia Angell, M.D., "Women in Medicine: Beyond Prejudice," *The New England Journal of Medicine*, Vol. 304, pp. 1161–1162, May 1981. Reprinted by permission of *The New England Journal of Medicine*.

Pages 171–172, by permission of Richard C. Proctor, M.D.

Pages 172–174, by permission of John M. Rhodes, M.D.

Page 178, by permission of Aaron T. Beck, M.D., Director, Center for Cognitive Therapy, 133 South 36th St., Philadelphia, PA 19104.

Page 182, photo by Mary Cairns/ADVERTISING AGE.

Pages 192–193, Michael C. Jensen, "Management: Using Meditation to Unwind," *The New York Times*, June 11, 1976. Copyright © 1976 by The New York Times Company. Reprinted by permission.

Pages 195–197, adaptation of The Relaxation Response (pp. 114–115) in *The Relaxation Response*, by Herbert Benson, M.D., with Miriam Z. Klipper. Copyright © 1975 by William Morrow and Company, Inc. By permission of the publishers.

Pages 203–207, Meyer Friedman, M.D. and Ray H. Rosenman, M.D., *Type A Behavior and Your Heart*. Reprinted by permission of Alfred A. Knopf, Inc., a division of Random House.

# INDEX

Heart rhythm, 58, 61, 72–75
Heart size, hypertension and increased, 77, 78
Heartburn, 83, 85, 86, 89
Helplessness, feeling of:
    irritable bowel and, 91
    as source of stress, 25
    of Type A individuals, 71–72
Hemorrhages:
    headaches as symptoms of cerebral, 103
    peptic ulcers and internal, 94
Heredity:
    coronary heart disease and, 61
    hypertension and, 79
    irritable bowel and, 90
    peptic ulcers and, 95
    (See also Predisposition)
Herniated (ruptured; slipped) disk, 108–110
Hersh, S. P., 19–20, 156–157
High-fiber diet for irritable colon, 91, 92
Hobbies for relaxation, 174, 176
Holiday headaches, 103
Hollister, Leo E., 123, 125–126
Holmes, Thomas H., 50, 52–54
Holmes-Rahe Life Event-Stress Scale, 50–54
Homeostasis, 42–44
    altruistic egoism and, 177
    disturbed, irritable bowel and, 89–90
Hormones, 45, 48, 69, 120
    migraine and changes in level of, 105
    (See also specific hormones, for example: Gluca-
      gon; Insulin)
Hostility, 75
    clinically standardized meditation for, 199
    diarrhea and suppressed, 172
    hypertension and, 80
    in Type A individuals, 206–207
    (See also Anger and frustration)
Hot and cold applications:
    for backache, 113
    for neck pain, 117
Hot shower for headaches, 106
Howard, John H., 25
Humor, competent copers' sense of, 174
Hunger as survival mechanism, 44
Hunter, John, 59
Hydrochloric acid (gastric juice), 84, 85
    indigestion and excess, 87
    peptic ulcers and, 94–95

Hyper-reactors (pre-hypertensives), 81
Hypertension, 1, 14, 16, 75–81, 97
    depression and, 80
    faulty adaptive reactions and, 49
    headaches and, 76
    heart attacks and, 61, 68–69, 75
    as silent killer, 76–79
    therapy for, 17, 77, 81, 106, 195, 198, 202
Hyperventilation, anxiety and, 122, 123
Hypoglycemia, 42

Illness and injury, 7–8, 20, 22, 25, 26, 51–53
    anxiety due to, 121
    irritable bowel due to, 91
    on scale of stress factors, 51, 53
    among Type A individuals, 65
Incidence:
    of backache, 107
    of coronary heart disease, among women execu-
      tives, 163, 164
    of depression, 136
    of headaches, 101–104
    of irritable bowel syndrome, 89
    of peptic ulcers, 92–93
Indigestion (dyspepsia; upset stomach; acid indiges-
    tion), 86–89
    due to depression, 139
    (See also Digestion)
Individual differences (see Personality)
Individual goals, company expectations vs., as source
    of stress, 21–22
Individual-related stress factors (see Personal prob-
    lems)
Infections, irritable bowel syndrome due to, 91
Infectious diseases, eradication of, 7
Injury (see Illness and injury)
Insecurity of Type A individuals, 65
Insight-oriented psychotherapy, 144
Insomnia (see Sleep, disturbances of)
Insulin, 43, 45
Internal balance (see Homeostasis)
Internal hemorrhaging due to peptic ulcers, 94
Intestinal obstruction, indigestion and, 86
Irritability, 1, 2, 6, 37
    anxiety and, 121
    caffeine intake and, 146
    depression and, 138

Memory, effects on (*Cont.*):
    of depression, 138
    of electroconvulsive therapy, 142
    of sensory deprivation, 43
   relaxation with a, 191–192
   selective, of unpleasantness, 179
Meningitis, headaches as symptoms of, 103
Menninger, Karl, 64
Menninger, William, 64
Menstrual distress, 202
Mental function:
   anxiety and, 123
   depression and, 138
   (*See also* Concentration difficulties; Memory)
Mental illness:
   societal view of, 14, 119
   (*See also* Depression; Neuroses; Phobias; Psychoses; Schizophrenia)
Meyer, Adolph, 50, 67
Michaels, R. R., 195
Middle-level executives, 20–23, 27–28
Midlife crisis (midlife transition), 33–37
Migraine headaches, 14, 49, 103–106, 108, 201–202
Miller, Neal E., 200–201
Mind, the (*see* Psyche)
Modeling for Type A behavior modification, 207
Modern society, 29–31
   anomie in, 29, 30
   egoism in, 30, 31, 34
   stressors of, 9–10
Moen, Phyllis, 151–152
Mood disturbances, depression and, 138, 139
Morgan, William P., 185
Mucus coating of stomach, ulcers and alteration in, 95
Muscle(s):
   in alarm reaction, 40
   electromyogram biofeedback for, 202
   relaxation of: based on muscle-mind relationship, 190–191
     for Type A behavior modification, 205
Muscle contraction headaches (*see* Tension headaches)
Muscle spasms (muscle tension), 13
   backache and, 110–112, 114
   exercise for, 184
   neck pain and, 115–116
Music as relaxation aid, 174, 183, 205

*Nature* (magazine), 47
Nausea, 172
   caffeine intake and, 146
   indigestion and, 86
   irritable bowel and, 89
   migraine and, 105
Neck pain, 5, 115–117
Nervous gut (irritable bowel syndrome), 83, 89–92
Neuroses, 32
*New England Journal of Medicine* (magazine), 164
*New York Times* (newspaper), 192–193
Newcomers, women executives facing problems of, 152–154
Nightingale, Florence, 45
Nitrite-containing foods, headaches and, 103
Norepinephrine, 195
Norpramin, 143
Noxious stimuli, effects of, 43–44

Obesity:
   atherosclerosis and, 78
   heart attacks and, 61
   hypertension and, 69, 80
*Occupational Health and Safety* (magazine), 21
Occupational level:
   and coronary heart disease among women executives, 163–164
   headaches and, 101–102
   peptic ulcers and, 92
Ordinary depression (blues), 37, 136–137
Organ language, effective coping and listening to, 171–172
Organizational structure as source of stress, 23, 26
Overeating, effects of, on digestion, 86, 87
Overwork syndrome, 172–174

Pain:
   abdominal: indigestion and, 86
     irritable bowel and, 89, 90
   backache, 112–114
   chest, 119, 121
   of muscle spasms, 111
   neck, 5, 115–117
   of peptic ulcers, 93–94
   stomach, respiratory alkalosis and, 122
   as survival mechanism, 44

Pain (*Cont.*):
  (*See also* Headaches)
Painting and sculpturing for relaxation, 174
Palpitations, 13, 43, 89, 122, 139
Paralysis, 202
Parent-child conflict, 10
Part-time work, 154–155, 160, 165, 166
Pasteur, Louis, 7
Pepsin, 94
Peptic ulcers (executive wound stripe), 1, 14, 16, 49,
    83, 92–98
  advice on how to get, 96–97
  anger-stimulated acidity and, 85
  backache and, 110
  duodenal, 49, 88, 93, 94
  gastric, 49, 93–94
  healing of, 95–97
  incidence of, 92–93
  indigestion and, 86
  symptoms of, 93
  therapy for, 97, 98, 195, 202
  among women executives, 153, 157
Peritonitis due to peptic ulcers, 94
Personal problems:
  as source of stress, 21, 22, 24–25
  (*See also specific types of personal problems,
      for example:* Alcohol abuse; Domestic
      problems)
Personality:
  anxiety and, 123
  and proneness to stress, 49–51
  and response to noxious stimuli, 44–45
  and response to stress, 14–15
  (*See also* Type A personality)
Personnel problems as source of stress, 27
Perspiration, irritable bowel syndrome and, 89
Pertofrane, 143
Phobias, biofeedback for, 202
Physical activity (*see* Exercise)
Physiological reactions to stress, 13, 40–48
  homeostasis and, 42–44
  and stages of response to stress, 47–48
Pituitary gland, 41, 47
Poisoning:
  food, 86
  uremic, 78
Power, need for, of Type A individuals, 69–70
Pre-hypertensives (hyper-reactors), 81

Predisposition, 49
  to anxiety, 123
  to depression, 139
  to irritable bowel, 90
  (*See also* Heredity)
Pressure, 1, 39–40
  alcohol consumption under, 60
  defined, 39
  individual differences in response to, 14–15
  modifying nature of, in anxiety therapy, 126
  self-imposed, Type A personality and, 66
  time, 21, 81
Prevalence of stress, 6–7
Primary (essential) hypertension, 79
Private stress factors (*see* Personal problems)
Proctor, Richard C., 140
Promotion (*see* Advancement)
Proneness to stress, personality and, 49–51
Propranolol for headaches, 106
Psyche:
  effects of, on gastrointestinal tract, 83–86, 95
  relationship between heart and, 59
  relaxation technique based on relation between
      muscles and, 190–191
  (*See also* Emotional stress)
Psychological stress (*see* Emotional stress)
*Psychology Today* (magazine), 16
Psychoses, 31
Psychotherapy, 208–209
  for anxiety, 125, 209
  behavior-centered, 144
  cognitive therapy, 178–179
  for depression, 141–144, 208–209
  group, 144
  insight-oriented, 144
  for irritable bowel syndrome, 92
  for peptic ulcers, 97–98
Pulse rate, effects on:
  of adrenalin, 45
  of caffeine, 146

Rahe, Richard H., 51–54
Rakel, Robert E., 127
Rapid eating, effects of, 87
Rashes, skin, 5, 50, 172
Recall (*see* Memory)
Recognition, lack of, as source of stress, 26

Reentry programs:
    for women doctors, 165, 166
    for women executives, 161
Regular vacations, effective coping with, 174
Regularity as basis for stress-free living, 31
Reisman, David, 30
Relaxation, 189–199
    aids for, 174, 176, 183, 185, 205
    with breathing techniques, 188–190
    with meditation (*see* Meditation)
    with a memory, 191–192
    muscle, for Type A behavior modification, 205
    progressive, 190–191
    to reduce cigarette smoking, 88
    with relaxation response, 193–198
    (*See also* Exercise)
Relocation, 10, 22, 121, 155
    on scale of stress factors, 50, 53
Resistance stage of response to stress, 49, 50
Respiratory alkalosis, anxiety and, 122
Rhoads, John M., 172–174
Rickels, Karl, 123
Rosenman, Ray H., 65, 67, 203, 206–207
Rubdown for backache, 113
Running, 184, 188
Ruptured (herniated; slipped) disk, 108–110

St. Martin, Alexis, 83–84
Salt intake, hypertension and, 79
Schizophrenia, 184
Schwartz, Gary E., 16–17
*Sciences, The* (magazine), 66
Sedatives (*see* Tranquilizers)
Sedentary living:
    atherosclerosis and, 78
    coronary heart disease and, 187, 189
    heart attacks and, 61
    overwork and, 173
Self-awareness, effective coping with, 169–171
Self-esteem, 22
    in depression, 138, 142
    of Type A individuals, 65, 66
Self-evaluation for Type A behavior modification, 205–206
Self-imposed pressure, Type A behavior and, 66
Self-imposed stress, Type A behavior and, 64

Self-observation for Type A behavior modification, 204–205
Selye, Hans, 45–49, 176–178
Sensitivity to light, migraine and, 105
Sensory deprivation, effects of, 43
Sensory disturbances (visual disturbances), 43, 139, 172
Separation (*see* Divorce and separation)
Severe depression (*see* Depression)
Sexuality, 6, 37, 65, 75, 139
Sheftel, Fred, 102
Shock, indigestion due to, 87
Shortness of breath, 77–78, 122
Side effects of antidepressants, 143
Sinequan, 143
Single women executives, 155
Sinusitis, 49
Skin rashes, 5, 50, 172
Skinner, James E., 61
Sleep:
    disturbances of, 6, 13
        anxiety and, 121, 130
        depression and, 139, 141, 142
        faulty adaptive reactions and, 49
        with irritable bowel, 89
        therapy for, 195, 202
    effective coping with regular, 174
    effects of exercise on, 185, 187
Sleeping pills, 121
Slipped (herniated; ruptured) disk, 108–110
Slowing down in Type A behavior modification, 205
Smoking (*see* Cigarette smoking)
Society:
    mental illness as viewed in, 14
    (*See also* Modern society)
Spasms (*see* Muscle spasms)
Sports (*see* Competitive sports; Exercise)
Spouse:
    communication with, 33, 37, 175
    reaction to death of, 51–52, 60, 74
Sprague, Eugene, 57–58
State anxiety, 122–123
Stereotypes of women executives, 156–158
Stereotypical attitudes toward women executives, 154–156
Stimulants (uppers), 6, 173
    (*See also* Caffeine intake)
Stimuli, noxious, effects of, 43–44

Type A personality (*Cont.*):
  heart attacks and, 61–65
  interplay between stress, heart attacks, and, 68–72
  modification of, 88–89, 202–207
  pathogenic core of, 66
  testing concept of, 67–68
Type B personality, 67–69, 71


Ulcers (*see* Peptic ulcers)
Uncertainty as source of stress, 1, 23–26
Unemployment (*see* Job loss)
Uppers (stimulants), 6, 173
  (*See also* Caffeine intake)
Urban violence, stress of, 9
Uremic poisoning, hypertension and, 78
Urgency, sense of, as source of stress, 25


Vacations, competent coping and need for, 173
Vagus nerve, hydrochloric acid secretion and overactive, 95
Valium (diazepam), 125, 131–133
Value system, stress and changing, 10, 11
Vegetables causing indigestion, 86
Violence, stress of, 9
Visual disturbances, 43, 139, 172
Vomiting, 105, 122, 146, 172


Walking, 184, 188, 205
*Wall Street Journal* (newspaper), 155
Warshaw, Leon J., 153, 188, 190
Weakness:
  in hypertension, 76
  with irritable bowel syndrome, 89
Western Collaborative Study Group, 68
White, Paul Dudley, 184

Widowers, death among, 51–52, 60, 74
Wives (*see* Spouse)
Wolf, Stewart G., 50, 85
Wolff, Harold G., 44, 85
Women, Type A, coronary heart disease among, 68
Women doctors, 164–166
Women executives, 151–164
  conflicts facing, 159–162
  coronary heart disease among, 162–164
  depression among, 158–159
  number of, 152
  special challenges facing, 152–156
  stereotypes of, 156–158
  workweek of, 19
"Women in Medicine: Beyond Prejudice" (Angell), 164
Woodchopping for relaxation, 185
Work:
  executive, defined, 19
  overwork syndrome, 172–174
  part-time, 154–155, 160, 165, 166
  (*See also* Advancement; Devotion to work; Executive stress; Occupational level; Reentry programs; *entries beginning with term:* Job)
Work relationship, unsatisfactory, as source of stress, 23–24
Workaholics:
  Type A individuals as, 65
  (*See also* Devotion to work)
Working mothers:
  number of (1980), 151, 153
  (*See also* Women executives)
Workload as source of stress, 21, 25, 27
Workweek of executives, 19
Worthlessness, feeling of, anxiety and, 121
Wright, Irving S., 59–60


Zloty, R. B., 187